MODERN TIMES

The League of Nations and UNO

S. R. Gibbons
P. Morican

LONGMAN

LONGMAN GROUP LIMITED
Longman House
Burnt Mill, Harlow, Essex, UK

© *Longman Group Limited 1970*

First published 1970
Ninth impression 1981

ISBN 0 582 20438 0

Printed in Hong Kong by
Sheck Wah Tong Printing Press Limited

Acknowledgements

We are grateful to the following for permission to reproduce copyright material: The British Council of Churches for a poem 'I am the World's Surplus Man' from *Christian Aid News*; Faber & Faber Ltd. for 'Conquerors' from *The Haunted Garden* by Henry Treece; Faber & Faber Ltd. and Random House Inc. for 'Refugee Blues' from *Collected Shorter Poems 1927–1957* by W. H. Auden, Copyright 1940, renewed 1968 by W. H. Auden; George G. Harrap Ltd. for an extract from *Now Thrive the Armourers* by R. O. Holles; International Labour Organisation for an extract from *Partners for Progress*; *The New York Times* for a Special Cable by Edwin L. James from issue dated 17th January 1920, Copyright © 1920 by The New York Times Company; Scorpion Press Ltd. for 'Your Attention Please' by Peter Porter; UNESCO for extracts from the League of Nations Bulletins of December 1931 and April 1946; Weidenfeld and Nicolson and Harper & Row Inc. for an extract from *No High Ground* by Fletcher Knebel and Charles W. Bailey, Copyright © 1960 by Fletcher Knebel and Charles W. Bailey.
For permission to reproduce photographs we are grateful to the following: Trustees of the British Museum and League of Nations' Document C.235M 95.1927vi *Question of Slavery*, page 25; Trustees of the British Museum and The League of Nations *Report Recommending the Adoption of a Unified System of Road Signs*, page 24; *Daily Mail*, pages 129, 143 and 155; *Daily Mirror*, pages 57, 77 and 129; Food and Agricultural Organisation, pages 99, 100 (below) and 101; the *Guardian* and Reuter, page 95; *Illustrated London News*, pages 47 (above), 51 (above and below), 59 (above), 63 (above) and 66; Imperial War Museum, pages 4 (below), 5 (above and below), 19, 75 and 159; *John Bull* (27 February 1932), page 49 (right); Keystone Press Agency Ltd, page 65 (above), 69 (above) and 90 (centre); League of Nations Document A.4.1926 (special) *Admission of Germany to the League of Nations*, page 30; League of Nations *Greek Refugee Settlement*, 1926 II 32, pages 20, 22 (below) and 32; League of Nations *Statistics Concerning the Imports and Exports of Raw Opium*, page 26; London Express Pictures, pages 2, 49 (left) and 149; Mansell Collection, page 69 (below); the *Observer*, pages 135 (right) and 141 (below); *Punch*, page 161; Radio Times Hulton Picture Library, pages 1, 4 (above), 31, 34, 60, 61, 127, 131 and 132 (above); *The Tatler*, 26 March 1919, page 10; United Nations, pages 79, 90 (left), 102 (left), 108 (right), 114 (above), 116 (above left), 137, 139 (above and below), 141 (above), 144, 145, 146, 150 (above and below), 158 and 160; United Nations High Commissioner for Refugees, pages 104 (below), 109 (left and right) 116–117 (right) and 117 (below left), United Nations International Children's Emergency Fund, page 114 (below); United Nations Relief and Works Agency, pages 104 (above), 106, 107, 111 (left and right) and 116 (middle left); United Press International (UK) Ltd, page 70. The illustrations on pages 38, 40, 52, 56 (above and below), 63 (below), 65 (below), 125 (above) and 157 (above) are David Low cartoons by arrangement with the Trustees of the Evening Standard; that on page 11 is © by the New York Times Company, reprinted by permission; that on page 157 (below) is the © of Papas; that on page 68 is the © of Manfred Rommel; the illustration on page 41 is taken from Newman *Danger Spots of Europe*, Right Book Club 1939; that on pages 28 and 135 (left) from WGJ Knop *Beware of the English* © Hamish Hamilton, 1939; and those on pages 53, 54 and 55 are from *Volkischer Beobachter*

Contents

Contents

Preface

The story of the two great international organizations runs like a continuous thread through the last half century, and its importance to the contemporary world is obvious. Our aim has been to present the essentials of this story in a way that will be appropriate to the average secondary school pupil.

The political side of League and UNO work, and the all-important attitudes of the Great Powers, have naturally taken up much of the available space. Nevertheless, we have also been at pains to indicate the tremendous advances which have taken place in the other, less publicized, aspects of internationalism in the twentieth century: co-operation for social and humanitarian purposes.

To reinforce the appeal of the subject matter we have made much use of the illustrative material available. We have also simplified those sections where simplification seemed justified, as, for example, the two World Wars, which are adequately treated elsewhere as separate topics. Similarly, of the many thousands of problems coming before the League or UNO we have necessarily included only those which at the time of writing seemed most important or most representative.

We acknowledge gratefully the help given by the following: the Embassy of Japan; the Embassy of Switzerland; the Swiss National Tourist Office; the United Nations Information Centre, London, and particularly Miss B. M. Nicholls, for permission to use and aid in selecting a wide range of photographs. Stanley Gibbons, Ltd., who kindly supplied stamps relevant to the League of Nations; D. Blake, P. Bedford, Teng Shou-hsin and R. Hunt for translations from Italian, German and Chinese originals; and D. Hurd, J. Foard, S. Hale and M. Draper for their valuable advice and comments.

S. R. Gibbons
P. Morican

1 The Setting up of the League of Nations

President Wilson in Europe

The French port of Brest had never before seen such a day. Ten American battleships lay outside the harbour. Huge crowds thronged the streets. Flags and bunting waved everywhere. Sailors lined the rigging of every nearby vessel as the tender brought the distinguished visitor ashore.

There was a brief welcome from the mayor, in a specially constructed pavilion, when the visitor was told that hopes for a peaceful world rested on him. Then came the procession, through rank after rank of cheering people. It was the first time an American president had ever visited Europe whilst in office, and Woodrow Wilson was touched to see how enthusiastic the people were. Four years of war might have left them jaded and weary, but their hopes for the future were boundless and somehow these centred on the President of the United States.

It was the same in Paris, and then in London. Although it was less than two months since the armistice which ended the Great War not even the British Prime Minister himself, Lloyd George, could have counted on such a tumultuous reception. For to many simple honest folk, Woodrow Wilson seemed to

President Wilson and his wife. Wilson's visit to Europe at the end of 1918 was a tremendous personal triumph

Daily Express

NO. 5,889.　　　LONDON, FRIDAY, DECEMBER 27, 1918.　　　ONE PENNY.

WONDERFUL WELCOME TO PRESIDENT WILSON.

TRIUMPHAL PROGRESS THROUGH ENORMOUS CROWDS.

UNPRECEDENTED SCENES.

President Wilson received a magnificent welcome from London. It marked the proudest and happiest moments in the relations between the two great English-speaking democracies.

CLIMAX OF ENTHUSIASM.

FIERCE STREET FIGHTING IN BERLIN.

SAILORS IN IMPERIAL PALACE ATTACKED WITH ARTILLERY AND MACHINE GUNS.

By H. J. GREENWALL,
"Daily Express" Special Correspondent.
BERLIN, Dec. 25.

MRS. WILSON'S HATS MR. WILSON IN AND GOWNS. DOWNING STREET.

DAILY SHOPPING ROUND IN PARIS.

TO-DAY'S CONFERENCES ON ALLIED POLICY.

"Daily Express" Correspondent.
PARIS, Dec. 25.

MRS. WILSON,

PALACE STORMED.

At the Chancellor, Dec. 24.

SIR E. GEDDES' DEPUTY.

LORD LYTTON IN CHARGE OF NAVAL PEACE QUESTIONS.

The Prime Minister has appointed the Earl of Lytton an additional parliamentary Secretary to the Board of Admiralty, in order that he may act as deputy to the First Lord, Sir Eric Geddes, in connection with naval policy which may arise in connection with the Peace Conference.

SPEECH AT DOVER

have an answer to the deepest, most urgent of human problems: how to abolish war. 'Merely to win the war was not enough,' he said in Paris, 'it must be won in such a way as to ensure the future peace of the world.' This, he told his eager audiences, must be through a League of Nations. The peoples of the world must act together to prevent the outbreak of wars, to solve the problems of the nations which always before had been settled on the battlefield. 'There is a tide running in the hearts of men . . .' he told one of his London audiences, and indeed there was. Men all over the world were determined that the awful horrors of 1914 should, if humanly possible, be prevented from happening again.

The President, together with others who had similar ideas of a great League of Nations to secure peace, carried with them the hopes of millions.

The War to End Wars

Conquerors: HENRY TREECE

By sundown we came to a hidden village
Where all the air was still
And no sound met our tired ears, save
For the sorry drip of rain from blackened trees
And the melancholy song of swinging gates.
Then through a broken pane some of us saw
A dead bird in a rusting cage, still
Pressing his thin tattered breast against the bars,
His beak wide open. And
As we hurried through the weed-grown street,
A gaunt dog started up from some dark place
And shambled off on legs as thin as sticks
Into the wood, to die at least in peace.
No one had told us victory was like this;
Not one amongst us would have eaten bread
Before he'd filled the mouth of the grey child
That sprawled, stiff as a stone, before the shattered door.
There was not one who did not think of home.

The savagery and heartburn of the war are revealed in these pictures. Around the world wandering refugees, scarred buildings, and stone memorials constantly called to mind its horror. Profoundly shaken, war-weary people everywhere fastened their hopes on the proposed League of Nations as a means of ensuring that a war of the magnitude of 1914–18 would never occur again. *Above*: the price of war. Must Mankind continue to pay it? Each stone represents someone's father, brother or son. *Below*: the reality of war.

Many towns and villages were damaged as extensively as this one. Ville-sur-Ancre main street

Home on a waggon. Thousands of families lost their homes and were forced to trundle the roads like this

The League Takes Shape

The idea of a 'league of nations' had crystallized as the full meaning of war in the twentieth century had become obvious to all. By 1915 League of Nations societies existed in Britain, the United States and France. The British Society had the support of the Prime Minister, Mr Asquith, and the American one was led by a former president, W. Taft. In 1917 the Pope issued a message supporting the League idea, and statesmen like Smuts of South Africa and Lloyd George in Britain mentioned it often in speeches. Early in 1918 it became one of the main war aims of the United States, being the last and most important of the famous 'fourteen points' of President Wilson.

When the war was at last over General Smuts made some practical suggestions about the way the League should be organized and run. In a far-seeing pamphlet he made it clear that he thought of the League as a great step forward in the world's history. It should be designed to control all the international affairs of the nations. Trade, transport, co-operation, disputes and disagreements—the League should discuss, regulate and settle them all, a sort of parliament for future nations.

Others had been thinking along the same lines, especially, of course, Woodrow Wilson. When the Peace Conference met in January 1919 he asked that the setting up of the League should have priority and not be put on one side for later. There was speedy agreement on this, and a committee set to work to produce a 'covenant'—a sort of international agreement and rule book which all member states would have to sign.

With Wilson as its chairman the committee made rapid progress; by April 1919 the Covenant was ready. Wilson brought it before a meeting of the Peace Conference and it was accepted. It would come into force as soon as the final treaty of peace was signed. Sir Eric Drummond was made the first Secretary-General, and the home of the League was fixed as Geneva. Sir Eric dashed off to London to start building up the organization and appointing a truly international staff.

The League Comes to Life

The first meeting of the new-born League was held in Paris in January 1920. It came shortly after the Treaty of Versailles had at last been signed between the Allied and Central Powers which had fought the Great War. Not till the end of the year did the League move to Geneva, and even then it had to wait some time for its permanent home to be built.

The first session of the League of Nations was a solemn and wonderful occasion, but there was one tragic feature. So far President Wilson, whose ideals had fired the hopes of so many millions, had failed to persuade the American Senate to accept and ratify the Peace Treaty. The United States was still officially at war with Germany, and outside the League of Nations. Wilson's chair was empty.

SPECIAL CABLE TO THE NEW YORK TIMES

By Edwin L. James: Paris, January 16th.

The League of Nations is a reality. Modestly and democratically, it began to function this morning at 10.30 o'clock, when the Executive Council opened its first meeting in the clock room of the French Foreign Ministry.

Nine men gathered about a green covered table in one end of the salon of crimson and gold and put in motion the machinery of the most ambitious experiment in government man has ever essayed, while a hundred or more diplomats from the four corners of the earth looked on.

Leon Bourgeois was president at this meeting. He spoke immediately of the absence of the American President. The duty of being chairman, he said, 'should have fallen to President Wilson. We respect the reasons which will delay the final decisions of our friends in Washington, but we may all express the hope that the difficulties will soon be overcome, and that a representative of the great American Republic will occupy the place which awaits him among us.'

The Council went on to appoint a commission to fix definitely the frontier between the Saar and Germany. This was the only item of business for that first session, but it was the foretaste of a great deal to come. The League of Nations was a going concern.

The Search for Peace through the Ages

The statesmen of the twentieth century who brought the League idea to life were not the first to think on these lines. The problem of war has been with us always, and the threat it presents to

7

civilization and culture is obvious. Below in diagram form are shown some of the stages by which the nations moved towards international action in the century before 1920.

Long before the nineteenth century there were thinkers who saw the problem clearly and suggested remedies, For the most part they were lone voices, far ahead of their times, but some of their ideas are nowadays more familiar to us. Some of their proposals remain dreams for the future. Here are some of the most important:

DANTE ALIGHIERI, the Italian poet, suffering continually from the feuds and minor wars of medieval Italy, suggested in his book *The Kingdom* (1309) that a common law was needed which should be binding on all nations. It was to be the better part of six centuries before this vital idea was to make any real progress towards practice.

Man's efforts to stem the floodtide of war: the growth of international action since the Napoleonic Wars. So far, the work is still far from complete, but with the League and UNO the nations have at least started to build in earnest

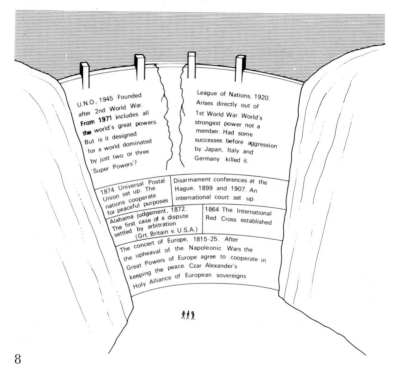

U.N.O., 1945 Founded after 2nd World War. From 1971 includes all the world's great powers. But is it designed for a world dominated by just two or three 'Super Powers'?

League of Nations, 1920. Arises directly out of 1st World War. World's strongest power not a member. Had some successes before aggression by Japan, Italy and Germany killed it.

1874 Universal Postal Union set up. The nations cooperate for peaceful purposes

Disarmament conferences at the Hague, 1899 and 1907. An international court set up.

Alabama judgement, 1872. The first case of a dispute settled by arbitration (Grt. Britain v. U.S.A.)

1864 The International Red Cross established

The concert of Europe, 1815-25. After the upheaval of the Napoleonic Wars the Great Powers of Europe agree to cooperate in keeping the peace. Czar Alexander's Holy Alliance of European sovereigns

ERASMUS, the Dutch scholar famous for his work on the Greek New Testament, suggested an International Court composed of 'Righteous Men' which would have the task of settling international disputes. His book *The Complaint of Peace* (1517) sketches out his advanced ideas in some detail.

SULLY, a French Duke and powerful politician, proposed the creation of a 'World Army', with different nations contributing groups of men (1595).

HUGO GROTIUS, another great Dutchman, is generally regarded as 'the father of international law', about which he wrote extensively. In 1625 he produced his book *Of the Law of War and Peace*. This laid a firm foundation of ideas and principles on which others were later to build. 'Laws must apply to nations as well as to individuals', he said.

WILLIAM PENN, the Quaker after whom Pennsylvania was named, wrote about the advantages of European Federation. He put forward the notion that there should be 'international languages'. He suggested Latin and French as the most suitable (1693).

J. J. ROUSSEAU, French philosopher, again puts forward the idea of an international army which would back up the work of an international court (1761).

IMMANUEL KANT, the German thinker who laid the basis of much modern philosophy, suggests the abolition of national armies. They would be replaced by a truly international law. He titles his book *On Everlasting Peace* (1795).

It is very significant that most of the advances that have been made towards international peace maintenance have arisen directly out of man's experience of the destructiveness of war. The 'Concert of Europe' in the years after 1815 was an attempt to achieve stability after the gigantic upheavals of the Napoleonic period. The founder of the Red Cross had been appalled by the experiences he had had when visiting Solferino, in northern Italy, just after a bitter battle in 1859. The 'Alabama judgment' arose out of the marauding activities of a British-built warship during the American Civil War. The League of Nations was the product of World War One, and the United

Nations Organization (UNO) of World War Two. It is no accident that these two organizations, by far the greatest steps forward so far taken, arose from the two most devastating conflicts which mankind has yet experienced.

The United States Turns its Back on the League

The year 1919 saw two tough political battles being fought— one in Europe, and one in the United States. In Europe the terms of the Peace Treaty were being hammered out at Paris, and the Germans opposed them as much as they dared. The Allies, however, held the whip hand, and their veiled (and sometimes quite open) threat of a resumption of the war would in the end force the Germans to sign. The battle was of a different kind altogether in the United States, where Senator Lodge led a bitter opposition to the treaty and to President Wilson.

At first it seemed that the Americans would approve the treaty and join the League, but as the weeks passed those who for one reason or another disliked the treaty joined forces and became more determined in their opposition. Many distrusted the way the United States seemed to be preparing to plunge into world—and especially European—politics, as a member

Through American eyes: *Left:* this cartoon from *The New York World* shows clearly that many Americans expected that opposition to the League would fail, and that it was an old-fashioned, 'stick-in-the-mud' attitude anyway.

Right: Republican opposition to the League appears here as a band of hostile Indians like those who attacked the Pilgrim Fathers long before

of the League. Others feared that as members American soldiers might find themselves fighting and dying in defence of the British or French empires, which they looked upon with a great deal of suspicion. Some, the German-Americans and the Irish-Americans, sympathized with the Germans over the terms of the treaty, or hated the British for their repression of Ireland, and opposed the treaty and the League for these reasons.

SEVEN VITAL VOTES

Wilson campaigned tirelessly for the endorsement of the treaty and for America's entry to the League. But on 2 October he had a serious paralytic stroke. He was a sick man from then on. When the treaty came to the US Senate in November his efforts were defeated. The treaty was rejected, and with it US membership of the League. This decision was reinforced the following March, when once again the President's enemies proved too strong. Just seven more votes and the necessary two-thirds majority would have been there. But they could not be found.

Europeans will find this difficult to understand. They often forget that the United States had long been accustomed to staying well outside the tangle of European politics. Americans distrusted the sudden plunge which they seemed to be taking into world affairs. Couldn't they stay out of it all and concentrate on developing their own great land? Many sincere Americans took this point of view.

The President's firmest supporters unwillingly helped to defeat the treaty and the League. A large number of alterations had been tacked onto the treaty by Senator Lodge and his allies. Wilson was stubborn about this and told his supporters not to ratify the treaty as it stood, with all the changes. He wanted it to be accepted with no alterations. His friends and his opponents therefore voted against accepting the treaty, though for quite different reasons. Lodge and the Republicans had outmanoeuvred him.

We can see now that those who kept the United States out of the League of Nations were wrong, though no doubt sincere. The League's chance of success in preventing wars was cut down enormously. It was a disaster, and the world was to pay for it.

Despite the blow, the work of establishing the League went ahead, though many doubted whether it could do any good without the United States as a member. Some still hoped that the unfortunate decision would one day be reversed. But the chances of this faded and disappeared, although the Americans did co-operate in some of the League's 'agency' work.

Woodrow Wilson, the man who had done so much to bring into being the first 'Parliament of all Mankind', died a disappointed man in 1924. But by then there was abundant evidence that the League would make its mark after all. Much had been lost; but not all.

The Palace of the Nations, Geneva

In March 1919 the following message was dispatched to the Paris Peace Conference: 'Switzerland would consider it a great honour to offer the hospitality of its territory should the League of Nations wish to establish its headquarters there.' This generous offer was accepted and Geneva became the headquarters of both the League of Nations and the International Labour Office.

The Palace of the League of Nations
is shown in this commemorative stamp

Feverish activities were necessary to prepare Geneva for its role as host to the international organization. There were few international telegraph and telephone facilities. No building was large enough to house all the members of the League Secretariat and the Assembly. Temporary accommodation was arranged and some of the larger hotels became offices and headquarters.

It was decided in 1926 to build a new permanent head-quarters. An international competition was arranged and architects from member states were invited to compete by submitting a plan for new buildings. There was no outright winner. Instead several plans were combined. Work started in 1929 and was completed in 1936.

The Palace of the Nations was located on a hillside commanding beautiful views of Lake Geneva and the Alps. It provided over seven hundred offices and many conference rooms. Many nations contributed to its construction and decoration. Here a floor was laid in Finnish granite, there walls and pillars faced with marble from Sweden. A Spanish artist executed a series of gold and sepia murals, an American contributed a huge sum of money for the library.

Geneva became the home of many servants of the League. Even after the end of the League many of the League buildings came to be used by agencies of the UN. Modernized for UN purposes the Palace of the Nations still remains an important headquarters for international operations.

2 Framework for Peace

How the League was Organized

These were the four main organs of the League:

THE ASSEMBLY

THE COUNCIL OF THE LEAGUE

THE SECRETARIAT OF THE LEAGUE

THE PERMANENT COURT OF INTERNATIONAL JUSTICE

The Assembly

The Assembly was the debating chamber
for the members.

All members had one vote each.

The Assembly admitted new members.

It elected non-permanent members
to the Council.

The Assembly voted the Budget.

The League of Nations and UNO
The Council of the League

The Council consisted of permanent and temporary members. In 1930 the five permanent members were Britain, France, Germany, Italy, Japan. Temporary members were elected by the Assembly for a period of three years. The number varied from four in 1920 to ten in 1936.

A member of the League affected by a discussion in the Council was entitled to temporary membership for the duration of such discussions. As a small body the Council could be summoned quickly and could take prompt action where it was needed.

The Secretariat of the League

The Secretariat was an international civil service carrying out the numerous administrative duties of the League. It was entrusted with the vital task of preparing reports for and keeping records of the Assembly and the Council.

There were many divisions to the Secretariat. Here are just four of them:

| Health | Armaments | Social Questions Drugs | Economic and Financial |

The Permanent Court of International Justice

Judges were chosen reflecting the world's different legal systems.

The Court was located at The Hague, Holland.

The Court would give a decision where two disputing parties requested it.

The Court also gave advice or guidance to the Assembly or Council on request, and performed the task of interpreting international treaties and conventions.

The International Labour Organization

The ILO was an association of the members of the League and had as its aim the improvement of conditions for workers all over the world. Included in the organization were also representatives of both employers and workers who worked side by side with the representatives of national governments.

The work of ILO was varied but always had the interests of workers in mind. Topics discussed were wage rates, conditions at work, safety, health hazards, employment of children and women, and schemes to combat unemployment.

Some positive results of ILO's work:
(*a*) International proscription of the use of white lead in paints
(*b*) A minimum age of employment for children

One of the several stamps issued in commemoration of the International Labour Organization

3 The League in Action

Getting the World Back to Normal : War Prisoners and Refugees

The aftermath of war always brings serious difficulties. Physical damage to buildings may eventually be repaired, or the buildings replaced. But some human problems are not so easily solved.

After World War One two such problems were the repatriation of prisoners and the welfare of refugees, people who had been forced to flee their homes during the fighting. The picture below gives a vivid impression of the size of the task that was handed to the League.

There were still many thousands of prisoners held in confinement who simply could not be turned free with no means of returning to their own country. During the war many had been kept in temporary camps and had received little attention from their hostile captors. Over two million German prisoners were

In the cages of Abbeville. Vast numbers of prisoners waited anxiously for their release

in temporary camps in Russia, where starvation and typhus were killing thousands weekly. Urgent medical and financial assistance was needed if these unfortunate men were to be saved and restored to their homelands.

The refugee problem was equally difficult and was made even worse in some parts by the minor wars that broke out after 1919. Where large numbers of homeless families streamed across war-torn frontiers there arose shanty towns built of timber and any other useful materials that could be found. With League help many of these people found homes.

Sometimes numbers were so great that the authorities could not cope with the pitiful tide of uprooted human beings, and emergency arrangements had to be made, like those in the illustration.

FRIDTJOF NANSEN

One of the great names associated with League of Nations work on refugees and prisoners is that of Fridtjof Nansen. Nansen was a Norwegian explorer who had attained fame by his activities in the Arctic.

When the League was established in 1919 Nansen was already fifty-eight, but he launched vigorously into the work of repatriating the many prisoners throughout the world.

Boxes in the Municipal Theatre in Athens. Each box houses a refugee family

Disinfectors at work in a large refugee camp. They were a vital part of the
equipment where large numbers were gathered together in poor conditions. The
danger of epidemics was a constant worry

Dinner time at Baranowicze camp, Poland. The eastern campaigns of 1914–18 and
the readjustment of frontiers on a vast scale resulted in untold human misery and
the destruction of ordinary home life for countless thousands

The League in action on the world refugee problem:
The Infectious Diseases Committee of the League of Nations provided this
ambulance for work among the shifting refugee populations

Victims of a disturbed world. Children in an eastern camp wait for their mothers
to return from queuing for a ration of milk

Although he had the support of the Council of the League, Nansen still felt that more urgency was required than the League could supply, and so he set up a special international fund, the 'Nansen Relief Fund', to provide enough money to give assistance to all the needy areas. In the space of a few years Nansen restored some 400,000 prisoners of thirty different nationalities to their homelands. As one commentator stated: 'There is not a country on the continent of Europe where wives and mothers have not wept in gratitude for the work Nansen did.'

A Thousand and One Activities

The activities of the League were many and varied. In the space of a few pages it would be difficult to describe them all. Here are a few examples of those activities to indicate their nature and the kind of detailed reports that were published.

The League reported on the marking of shipping channels in international waters and made recommendations.

BUOYS

Reproduced below and overleaf are parts of a page from a League publication dealing with tide markings and signals to identify moving vessels.

II TIDE AND DEPTH SIGNALS:

I State of tide

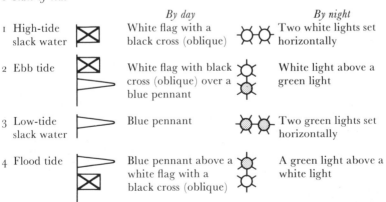

		By day	By night
1	High-tide slack water	White flag with a black cross (oblique)	Two white lights set horizontally
2	Ebb tide	White flag with black cross (oblique) over a blue pennant	White light above a green light
3	Low-tide slack water	Blue pennant	Two green lights set horizontally
4	Flood tide	Blue pennant above a white flag with a black cross (oblique)	A green light above a white light

2. Height of water

	Multiple of the unit (5 units)	Main unit (the metre for countries which employ the metric system)	Secondary unit (1/5th of the main unit for countries using the metric system)	Fraction of the secondary unit
By day Alternative A	Cylinder 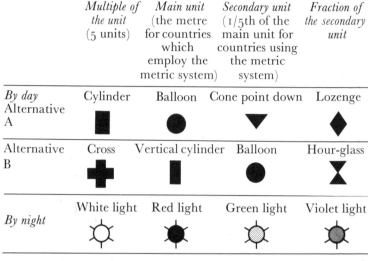	Balloon	Cone point down	Lozenge
Alternative B	Cross	Vertical cylinder	Balloon	Hour-glass
By night	White light	Red light	Green light	Violet light

The League investigated railway signalling on international routes. For motoring the League published its own 'highway code' with recommended international road signs and signals.

RAILWAY SIGNALS

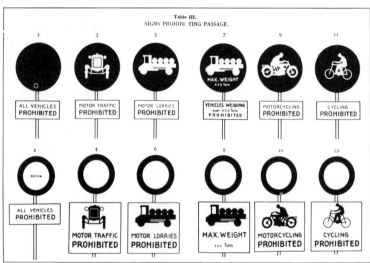

Table III.
SIGNS PROHIBITING PASSAGE.

1 ALL VEHICLES PROHIBITED
3 MOTOR TRAFFIC PROHIBITED
5 MOTOR LORRIES PROHIBITED
7 VEHICLES WEIGHING over xxx Tons PROHIBITED
9 MOTORCYCLING PROHIBITED
11 CYCLING PROHIBITED

2 ALL VEHICLES PROHIBITED
4 MOTOR TRAFFIC PROHIBITED
6 MOTOR LORRIES PROHIBITED
8 MAX. WEIGHT xxx Tons
10 MOTORCYCLING PROHIBITED
12 CYCLING PROHIBITED

Uniting for road safety: a page from the League's report recommending the adoption of a uniform system of road signs and signals on international routes

In 1924 a Slavery Commission was established by the League Council. It decided to ask members to co-operate in stamping out slave-dealing, either by sale, exchange, or 'gift'. Forced labour and doubtful 'adoption' measures were also to be reported. Despite its enquiries, however, the Commission was still mentioning the existence of slave dealings in its report of 1937.

The question of slavery: the government of the Sudan replies to the League's enquiries concerning the possible existence of slavery in the Sudan. All members of the League received similar letters of enquiry

---

LEAGUE OF NATIONS.

QUESTION OF SLAVERY.

COMMUNICATION FROM THE GOVERNMENT OF THE SUDAN.

Note by the Secretary-General:

The Secretary-General has the honour to circulate for the information of the Council and the Members of the League the following letter from the Government of the Sudan regarding the question of slavery.

Governor General's Office,
Khartoum, April 12th, 1927.

To the Secretary-General;

Under Article 7 of the Slavery Convention signed at Geneva on September 25th, 1926, the High Contracting Parties undertook to communicate to you the Laws and Regulations enacted by them with a view to the application of the provision of the Convention.

The Laws and Regulations made by this Government for the purpose of repressing slavery in the Sudan have already been communicated to you in my despatch No. 154 of August 29th, 1925[1], and have been published by the Foreign Office in London in a White Paper (Sudan No. 1, 1926).

2. Under Resolution 3, proposed in connection with Article 7 of the Convention, the Assembly of the League also requested the Council to prepare a document which, in addition to mentioning the Laws and Regulations referred to above, should include any supplementary information which might be furnished spontaneously by the Members of the League with regard to the measures taken by them to carry out these Regulations.

3. With a view to furnishing such information and fulfilling his undertaking to make full enquiry into the question of slavery in this country my predecessor, Sir Geoffrey Archer, in a letter quoted in the annex to Part 4 of the White Paper referred to above, appointed a special Commissioner to collate information on the subject and put forward recommendations to him for action likely to accelerate the total disappearance of slavery from the Sudan.

4. During the course of his investigations, the Commissioner was able to visit most of the Provinces concerned. Information regarding those areas which he was unable to visit was collected by enquiry from the administrative officials concerned.

5. The conclusions to which I have arrived as the result of his enquiries are as follows :

(*a*) Slavery in the Provinces north of Khartoum is moribund. The number of domestic slaves still living with their masters has been rendered insignificant, chiefly as the result of the publicity given to the possibilities of freedom and the increased opportunities for independent employment offered by various works that have been taken in hand by the Government and private enterprise.

(*b*) In the extreme south, that is to say in Bahr El Ghazal, Mongalla and Upper Nile Provinces, slavery may be said to be non-existent, as no slave owning communities exist there.

[1] Note by the Secretariat : See document A 69, 1925, VI communicated to the Council and the Members of the League on September 14th, 1925.

S. d. N. 575 (F.) 600 (A). 5/27. Imp. d'Ambilly.

The League of Nations and UNO

The League tried to engage the co-operation of members in controlling the traffic in dangerous drugs. It was most concerned that members should educate their peoples about the dangers of using them. League publications provided evidence of the origins and directions of the drug trade.

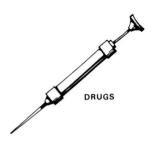

DRUGS

APPENDIX 2: IMPORTS AND EXPORTS OF RAW OPIUM Weights are given in kilos throughout			
	1918	1919	1920
China			
Imports	20,000 a	9,400 a	8,300 a *a* To territories under Japanese control only
Exports	—	—	
Japan			
Imports	11,000 bc	33,000 bc	30,000 bc *b* Large stock bought owing to cheap price
Formosa			
Imports	119,000	124,000	160,000 A sudden trade from the U.S.A. appears to have sprung up: in 1919 12,400 kilos, and in 1920 90,000 kilos; a fairly constant supply from Persia (about 25,000 kilos). The Indian supply fell to 9,000 in 1920 from a previous average of about ten times that amount
Chosen			
(Korea)	No information is given as to the import of opium		
Kwantung			
Imports	17,000	9,000	8,100 All Persian

For Japan, footnote c:

	1918	1919	1920	
c	1,700	1,370	2,260	from England
	9,400	10,700	—	from India
	—	21,000	28,000	from U.S.A.
	—	—	160	from Italy

Above: imports and exports of raw opium. A page which illustrates the kind of detailed statistical work that the League produced

The League's work for health and education is indicated in the publication of these stamps

Mandated and Trust Lands

It was decided by the victors in 1919 that the former colonies of Germany and Turkey should be confiscated. Britain and France acquired territory from Germany and Turkey in Africa and the Near East, while New Zealand, Australia and Japan divided up Germany's far eastern territories.

The Covenant of the League went on to establish a mandates system for the colonies. What this meant in effect was that the League gave to the allied powers who took over the colonies the special responsibility of governing them and promoting their development. Each year the ruling power was to report to the League on its trust territory, and this report was considered by a special Commission. A distinction was made between those territories expected to become self-governing fairly soon—mainly ex-Turkish—and those which by reason of their poor resources and backwardness needed to be administered as a trust territory for much longer. The latter were mainly ex-German colonies in Africa.

In German eyes the League was guilty of 'rubber-stamping' the arrangements of the Versailles Treaty, with its highly unpopular and violently anti-German clauses. This was one of the reasons why German hearts were for long hardened against the League. When Hitler came to power Nazi propaganda played continually on the theme of the lost German territories.

Some of the League of Nations trust territories

Mandated country	Former ruler	Mandatory power responsible to the League
Africa		
Togoland	Germany	France, Britain (Togoland was divided)
Cameroon	Germany	France, Britain (Cameroon was divided)
German South West Africa	Germany	Union of South Africa
Tanganyika	Germany	Britain
Near East		
Palestine	Turkey	Britain
Syria	Turkey	France
Iraq	Turkey	Britain
Far East		
Eastern New Guinea	Germany	Australia
Samoa	Germany	New Zealand
Nauru	Germany	Britain
Marshall Islands	Germany	Japan

B

The League of Nations and UNO

As seen through German eyes:
'London calling: England grows
stronger every day!'
The Nazis were intensely conscious
of the fact that Germany had lost all
her colonies, whereas the British
Empire seemed to grow ever stronger

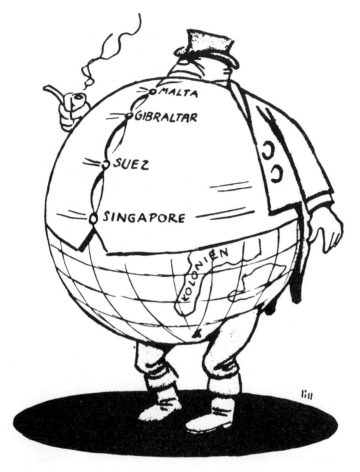

4 The Growth of the League

Germany: Europe's Biggest Question Mark.

It was essential, right from 1920, that the League of Nations should include Germany as soon as possible. So many European problems affected or concerned Germany and her economic strength was so great, and her position in central Europe so important, that sooner or later she must once again play a major part in world affairs.

1920 The Germans themselves demanded, in rather strong terms, to be one of the founder members of the League. The bitterness of the war years was still too strong, however. They were told to apply for membership when things had settled a little and it had become quite clear that they were carrying out the terms of the Versailles Treaty. At the first Geneva meeting Lord Robert Cecil stated very strongly that he did not wish the admission of Germany to the League.

1922 Lloyd George, the British Prime Minister, urged the entry of Germany. Like many others he realized that only when Germany and Russia had been brought back into normal relations with the rest of the world could there be any real hope of stability and progress. The Germans began to play 'hard to get'; while in France there was a new Prime Minister, Poincaré, who was completely opposed to German membership. The question was again put off.

1924 Ramsay MacDonald, the first Labour Prime Minister in Britain, declared his support for the League of Nations. Labour's election campaign had emphasized that a Labour government's foreign policy would be based on the Covenant of the League. MacDonald spoke in favour of German entry. The climate of opinion changed in France, too: Premier Herriot wanted the Germans in. The German Foreign Minister announced that Germany desired to enter the League at an early date.

1925 A great change in the international atmosphere seemed possible following the signing of the Treaties at Locarno. Germany and France resolved to accept the Versailles frontiers established in 1919.

1926 The announcement for which the world had been waiting: Germany applied for membership. Seven years after the end of the war member nations received an important note from the Secretary-General, see below.

1928 The Kellogg Peace Pact was signed by sixty-five nations. That so many nations were prepared to sign a document which condemned war was regarded as a turning point in the history of the twenties. Following close on the admission of Germany to the League it was hailed as the brightest hope for peace since the war.

League of Nations Special Document 10 February 1926.
Germany asks to join the League of Nations

[Distributed to the Council, the Members of the League, and the Delegates to the Special Assembly].

A. 4. 1926 **(Special)**
(C. 60. M. 34. 1926. VII.)

Geneva, February 10th, 1926.

LEAGUE OF NATIONS.

ADMISSION OF GERMANY TO THE LEAGUE OF NATIONS.

LETTER FROM THE GERMAN GOVERNMENT.

Note by the Secretary-General.

The following letter from the Minister for Foreign Affairs of the Reich, dated February 8th, 1926, is circulated to the Members of the League. The original text in German of the following letter is kept in the archives of the Secretariat and can be consulted by Members of the League.

[*Translation*]

Berlin, February 8th, 1926.

With reference to the German memorandum of September 1924 to the Governments represented on the Council, and to the German Note addressed to you on December 12th, 1924, and the reply thereto of the Council of the League dated March 14th, 1925, as well as to the Note of the other parties to the Locarno Treaties of December 1st, 1925, of which a copy is attached, I have the honour, in accordance with Article 1 of the Covenant of the League of Nations, to propose herewith, in the name of the German Government, the admission of Germany to the League of Nations. I beg you to put this proposal on the Agenda of the Assembly as soon as possible.

(*Signed*) STRESEMANN.

Russia and the League

At the end of the First World War the Russians found themselves isolated and cut off as a nation. They had to face the problem of civil war, for there were strong forces at work seeking to overthrow the Communist revolution and all it stood for. The Bolshevik or Red Army struggled with the 'white' armies of the 'counterrevolutionary' forces. For a time the western powers supported the 'whites' in the effort to destroy the Soviet government in Moscow. The British sent a fleet to the Baltic and an expeditionary force to north Russia. France and the United States contributed troops, in the effort to help overthrow the 'Reds'. It was all to no avail, for by the summer of 1920 the Bolshevik soviets (councils) were well in control throughout Russia. Small wonder that they regarded the West with suspicion and resentment.

Lenin: organizer and leader of the Russian communist revolution

The Russians needed very much to re-establish their links with the rest of the world, for progress passes by those who live in isolation. But this was bound to be difficult. Communist ideas were widely distrusted, and the efforts of the Communist International to foster revolution in other countries—mainly western ones—caused great ill-will. Western firms with goods or money in Russia had seen them confiscated without compensation. The revolutionary government had cancelled all debts owed abroad. In addition, the line of new states in Europe —Estonia, Latvia, Lithuania and Poland—could only mean that Russian contact with the rest of the world would in future be a more difficult and complicated affair. Only around the city of Leningrad did the Russians still have access to the Baltic and its direct trade routes to the West.

The new Russia did not welcome the League of Nations. The League was regarded at first as a club for the highly industrialized capitalist Powers of the West, where their immoral 'land-grabbing' would be endorsed by the smaller nations dependent on them. It was felt that Germany, if she were ever induced to

Agricultural experts of the League's Colonization Service cross the River Halmacyon in Macedonia. They reported on the agriculture of the area, which depended heavily on the rose-growing industry

become a member, would be persuaded to throw her weight against the USSR.

Chicherin, Russian foreign minister till 1929, hurled insults at the League and could hardly mention it without the heaviest sarcasm. Those at Geneva and elsewhere who believed in the League and worked for it suffered the stream of abuse in silence and waited and hoped for the Russian attitude to change. They knew that if it were to succeed the League must ultimately include most if not all of the world's great powers. Russia was as essential to the League as Germany or the United States.

As the nineteen-twenties went by the League gradually built up an impressive record of good work. It settled numerous small disputes, as well as some bigger ones, between nations. Its work for war prisoners commanded respect, in Russia as elsewhere. Its fight to help refugees, to stamp out disease or to stop the slave trade in women and children forced even its Russian critics to revise their views.

The European governments one by one recognized the Union of Soviet Socialist Republics, as the country was now called. Slowly the Russian attitude became less hostile. Here are some of the steps by which Russia moved towards eventual membership of the League of Nations, in 1934.

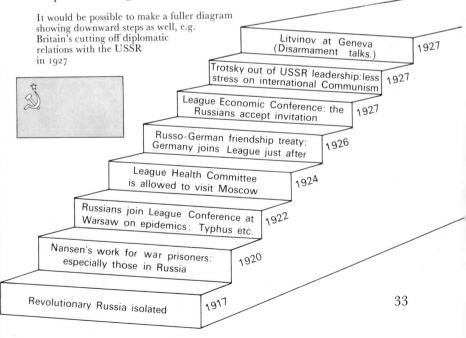

It would be possible to make a fuller diagram showing downward steps as well, e.g. Britain's cutting off diplomatic relations with the USSR in 1927

Litvinov at Geneva (Disarmament talks.) 1927

Trotsky out of USSR leadership: less stress on international Communism 1927

League Economic Conference: the Russians accept invitation 1927

Russo-German friendship treaty: Germany joins League just after 1926

League Health Committee is allowed to visit Moscow 1924

Russians join League Conference at Warsaw on epidemics: Typhus etc. 1922

Nansen's work for war prisoners: especially those in Russia 1920

Revolutionary Russia isolated 1917

33

The League at the Height of its Influence

The beginning of the nineteen-thirties saw the League facing the future with optimism. Membership had increased steadily. There was hope that the entry of the Soviet Union would not be long delayed, and the Russian Foreign Minister Litvinov was already a well-known figure at Geneva. There was steady co-operation with the United States, the one country whose goodwill and ultimate membership were vital for the success of any effort at world peace-keeping. An enormous variety of activities throughout the world was carried on through the League agencies, and reports were presented and statistics gathered on practically every problem that afflicted mankind. Hundreds of disputes and difficulties had been brought to Geneva for settlement, the majority of them successfully.

In many countries there had grown up League of Nations Associations, which did their best to make the good work widely known and discussed. Money was raised and forwarded to Geneva to assist in medical, cultural or scientific work throughout the five continents. Hundreds of thousands of ordinary people read the League's bulletins with interest and looked to Geneva to make the dream of a peaceful world come true.

Girls of Hampstead at a League of Nations Rally in Hyde Park, June 1921

Despite American isolationism, it seemed that the ideals of Woodrow Wilson and the other pioneers might be realized. It was possible to look back on the first ten or twelve years of the League's existence with pride and hope. At least there was a good basis from which to go on towards a final solution of the great problems of disease, intolerance, famine and war.

However, a glance at the accompanying diagram shows that four countries withdrew from the League during the fourteen year period up to 1934. Two of the four were great powers, with wide influence and great economic strength: Germany and Japan. Germany had come under Nazi control, and Japan had started her long struggle to wrest territory from China—aggression of the very type the Covenant was designed and framed to stop. But in 1933 the full effects of Nazi ideas and Japanese aggression were not yet obvious, and 1934 brought an official Soviet delegation to Geneva for the first time as a member. To acute observers the testing time for the new world organization had arrived; but success or failure still lay in the future.

Growth of the League of Nations, 1920–34

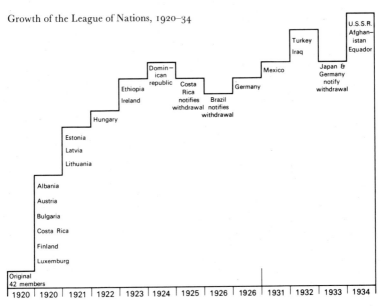

35

5 Problems for the League

The Attack on Corfu, 1923

A GENERAL IS MURDERED

Three powerful cars sped along a lonely road in northern Greece, near the town of Janina. The second car flew the flag of an Italian general, General Tellini. With him were two members of his staff, besides the driver and an interpreter. The first car contained Albanians, and the third Greeks.

The cars gradually became more and more separated. When the Albanians swished round a sharp bend beneath some tall trees they were probably at least a minute ahead, and the Greek car had fallen well behind.

Farnete, the Italian driver, approached the bend, and was suddenly startled to see an obstacle in the road: a tree trunk lay across the curve. He was forced to pull up sharply. A shattering, brutal hail of shots rang out from the cover on either side of the road. The five men in the car had no chance at all. Doctor Corti was killed in his seat. The others opened the doors but were shot down just outside the vehicle, General Tellini managing to stagger about twenty yards before collapsing into the ditch.

When the Greek car arrived, a minute or two later, it was all over, and the assassins had fled. General Tellini and his staff had been callously and cold-bloodedly murdered. The news was telephoned and telegraphed to the world. It reached Geneva as delegates were gathering for a meeting of the League Council.

CRISIS IN THE MEDITERRANEAN

General Tellini had been working on the instructions of the Conference of Ambassadors in Paris—a sort of council of four of the great powers which had won the First World War. (Its members were Britain, France, Italy and Japan.) Tellini's job was to mark out on the spot the frontier between Albania and Greece, and it was not made easier by the bad feeling on both sides. Who shot him we shall probably never know, for no

36

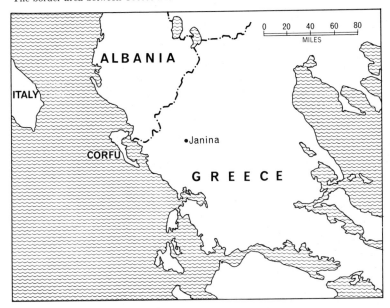

The border area between Greece and Albania and the Greek island of Corfu

trace of the murderers was ever found. They could equally well have been Greeks or Albanians.

The crisis developed fast. Mussolini, the new Italian Prime Minister who boasted of Italy's great strength, demanded a large payment of compensation from Greece. He insisted upon an enquiry to be completed in an impossibly short time, and the punishment of the guilty by execution. When the Greek reply was not to his liking Italian forces attacked the Greek island of Corfu, occupying it after a bombardment. War feeling ran high in both Italy and Greece.

In Geneva the Greek representatives had already placed the situation before the Council of the League. Excitement was intense, for no one needed reminding that only nine years earlier the Sarajevo murders had produced a very similar ultimatum to Serbia from Austria, and that this had led to world war within a matter of weeks.

The League in Geneva produced a plan to solve the crisis. It was sensible and fair, and only Italy refused to agree to it. Among other arrangements the Greeks were to place 50 million lire in a Swiss bank to await a final decision about the compensation demanded by Mussolini. But now arose a new problem:

37

'The New Member.' The Tellini murders and the Italian ultimatum to Greece strongly resembled the events which had led to world war in 1914

what to do about the Conference of Ambassadors, representing as it did the most powerful states in Europe?

A record of the Geneva meetings was sent to Paris, and from then on the Conference of Ambassadors took the lead and the League found itself reduced to the role of an adviser. Worse still, the conference altered the Geneva plan so that it was no longer fair but strongly biased against Greece and in favour of Italy. The Greeks, having agreed to abide by any decision, submitted with great bitterness and saw their 50 millions transferred to Italy. The Italian marines left Corfu.

The League had been designed to deal with just such a dangerous problem as this. It had acted promptly and fairly, and it had condemned the violence of the Italians. But it had lost the initiative when it had allowed the Ambassadors to impose their own decisions, and everyone knew that the Ambassadors had acted under pressure from Mussolini. The result was that a great power had once again got away with using force against a small power. However, a full-scale outbreak of war in the Mediterranean, which at one time seemed very possible, had been avoided.

38

1928: The Gun Smugglers

It was New Year's Day, 1928. The little town of Szent Gott-hard, on the frontier between Hungary and Austria, was as quiet and peaceful as usual. Many of the folk had been to church that morning, and were now getting on with the usual business of the day. Down at the railway station a row of trucks was lined up in a siding, waiting to be checked out by the Austrian customs men before crossing the border into Hungary. The lists showed that among the goods waiting to cross were sixty tons of MACHINE PARTS addressed to a transport agent in Hungary.

Normally the packing cases would not have been opened. But one of them was, and the telephone wires were soon humming with news that set off an international squabble. The sixty tons of machine parts were not quite correctly labelled! They were in fact MACHINE GUN PARTS.

THE QUESTIONS EVERYONE ASKED

Whose were these weapons? Where had they come from? Where were they destined for?

Was someone trying to break the Treaty of Trianon, which at the end of the First World War had limited the arms allowed to Hungary?

The problem came before the League, amid great excitement. Hungary's neighbours wanted to know whether the guns were meant for use against them. The Hungarians, meanwhile, had the machine gun parts broken up, and when the League's experts arrived at Szent Gotthard the task of tracing where they had come from had become almost impossible.

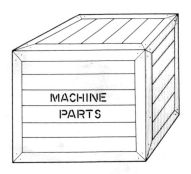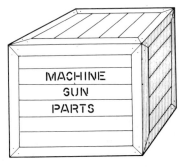

The trucks had started their journey at Verona, in Mussolini's Italy. The League could have asked for an explanation. But Italy was one of the great powers, and Mussolini was a man of violent and threatening temper if his actions were questioned. All through the League's discussions the Italian delegate sat quiet. He was not even asked for an explanation. The other great powers did not wish to embarrass Italy, and the small states feared to do so.

The League issued a general warning about arms smuggling and mildly rebuked the Hungarians. It had failed to use its powers fully and effectively, because it would not risk offending one of its founder members. How could the League earn respect if it did not act decisively whenever necessary? The Italians and the Hungarians had 'got away with it', and the world had been reminded that beneath the peaceful surface of Europe the dangerous old games of secret plotting and secret arming were still going on.

'The Devil's Toyshop'. The disposition of certain nations to increase rather than decrease their armaments in spite of all the pacts and pledges called for this cartoon of 'The Devil's Toyshop'. M. Briand, Sir Austen Chamberlain, President Coolidge and Signor Mussolini (representing in their persons France, Britain, United States and Italy) are not wicked lads, but weak. They are all fascinated by the hard shiny playthings and are drawn as usual to spend their Christmas pennies with kind old Mr Nick, who so understands children. 'Ah well, boys will be boys', he will say as they go outside and blow each other's heads off

Problems of Frontiers and Ownership
WHO OWNS WHAT?

Throughout the world there were in the nineteen-twenties and thirties numerous problems about territory. The frontiers between some states were in dispute and often became the scene of raids and 'incidents'. The maps overleaf show the areas where some of the worst disagreements existed.

Many of these disputes were ages old, and there seemed to be no easy solution. Many more had come into existence when the peace treaties after the First World War had carved up old states and made new ones on a scale unknown since the days of Napoleon. Here is a brief digest of some of the difficult 'who owns what' problems which came before the League; the numbers are those which mark the dispute on the following maps:

I. THE AALAND ISLANDS, 1920–21

Should these islands belong to Finland or to Sweden? The Aalanders wanted to be united with Sweden, but the League, after considering the previous history of the islands, decided that they should remain under Finnish control with the islanders' rights as a minority people carefully safeguarded by the League. Despite the disturbances created by the Second World War this has proved to be a satisfactory arrangement.

The redrawing of frontiers after 1918 had left problems all over Europe. Here the frontier has been fixed at a bridge, so traffic going from one part of the village to another must use the river!

Two of the boundary disputes which came before the League
1. The Aaland Islands, disputed by Sweden and Finland
2. Vilna, disputed by Lithuania and Poland, and coveted by Russia

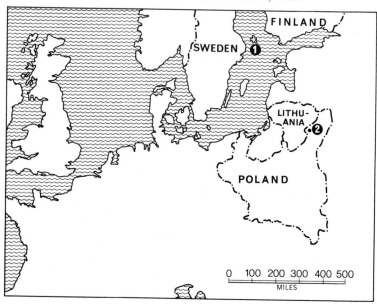

2. VILNA, 1920 ONWARDS

This was a particularly bitter quarrel about the ancient town of Vilna, which centuries before had been the capital of an independent Lithuania. Russia and Poland were both involved in the struggle for the city which started after the World War. The Poles were gravely disappointed when an independent Lithuania was again set up, and when the Lithuanians wanted to make Vilna their capital city once more they pointed out with justice that a very large majority of the people there were now Polish. A plan for a League of Nations force in the area came to nothing, and the Polish army which had seized the city remained in possession until the area was awarded to Poland by the Conference of Ambassadors.

3. MOSUL, 1924

Should this area, on the river Tigris, be within the new Turkey, or should it become part of the new state of Iraq? Many of the inhabitants were Kurds, a sturdily independent people who are still posing problems by their opposition to authority. If they were ruled by Iraq the task of absorbing and 'Turkifying' the other Kurds within the Turkish border would be made

The League tackles one of the many border disputes in the old Turkish Empire
3. Mosul, disputed by Turkey and Iraq

more difficult. The League investigated the problem at a special meeting, and the dispute was finally settled in favour of Iraq.

4. WAR IN SOUTH AMERICA: THE CHACO
One of the most bitter disputes which the League had to deal with concerned Bolivia and Paraguay. The two states wrangled unendingly about the Chaco, a vast, almost uninhabited area which separated them. In 1932 full scale war broke out, waged with weapons bought from up to a dozen other states, including Britain, the USA, France and Germany. The League did its best to arrange a ceasefire, and the commission which went to South America did a great deal to establish League prestige in that part of the world, but the war really came to an end when both Bolivia and Paraguay were too exhausted to continue.

5. THE LEAGUE FLAG ON THE AMAZON
Another South American dispute, this time between Colombia and Peru, was settled more promptly and more happily. An armed group of Peruvian patriots had captured a Colombian outpost at Leticia, and when Peruvian forts and warships began

43

The League tackles South
American border disputes
4. The Northern Chaco,
disputed by Bolivia and
Paraguay
5. Leticia on the Upper
Amazon, disputed by
Colombia and Peru

to take part the outlook for peace in South America seemed
very poor. But a change of ruler in Peru led to a change of heart;
the League's proposal for a League of Nations Commission to
govern the area for a year was accepted. The League flag flew
over Leticia, after which the rightful Colombian authorities
once more took over. The League's ability to deal with South
American, as well as European disputes had been effectively
shown.

6 Challenge

Japan Flouts the League

HARD TIMES FOR JAPAN

In 1931 Japan was facing serious economic difficulties. The worldwide slump in trade held the Japanese silk industry in its grip, and production in other fields was also dropping. But this downward swing in production and exports was not matched by a downward swing in the birth rate. The population was increasing at a rate that meant nearly a million extra mouths to feed every year.

The islands of Japan could not themselves provide the necessary food for this growing population. Because of the slump other countries did not now want the luxurious silk that Japan could offer in exchange for imports of food. Emigration could not solve the problem either, since the nearest non-Asian nations, the United States and Australia, had virtually forbidden the entry of Asians into their countries.

Earlier in the twentieth century the Japanese had acquired control of Korea, and with it railway rights that extended northwards into the Chinese province of Manchuria. With the growing economic difficulties some Japanese eyes turned towards Manchuria as a possible means of ending them. The army regiments in the province guarding the railway urged a military takeover.

THE JAPANESE ARMY

The attempts of the army officers to gain control of the government were a part of Japan's internal difficulties. Secret groups of them emerged with mysterious sounding names—'the Society of the Sword of Heaven' and the 'Blood Brotherhood'. These groups were pledged to increase the power of the army in state affairs. They believed that the army held the key to solving Japan's economic difficulties. It was the army that struck the blow against Manchuria and confronted the League with a positive act of aggression against one of its members.

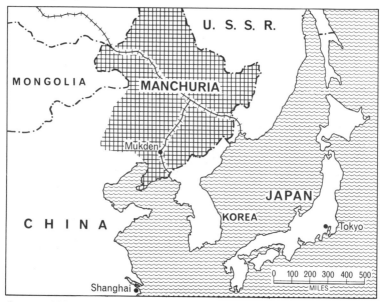

Japan and Manchuria, 1931. The railway line from Korea to Mukden was patrolled by Japanese troops

FLARE UP IN MANCHURIA: THE MUKDEN RAILWAY INCIDENT

Manchuria was Chinese but Japan had treaty rights to station troops along the railway line from Mukden to the Korean border. The Chinese had come to resent these treaty rights and planned eventually to squeeze the Japanese out of Manchuria completely. Friction occurred between the troops garrisoned in Mukden and the local population. In the summer of 1931 a Japanese soldier was killed in an incident with Chinese bandits.

The army became impatient with the government in Tokyo. The officers felt that they could soon quell any trouble from the Chinese in Manchuria. They also felt that Manchuria might provide some solution to Japan's economic difficulties. The army began to make its own plans.

The exact truth about the Mukden railway incident is still not known. At the time Japanese officers claimed that on 18 September 1931 they came across Chinese soldiers trying to blow up a section of the railway line which they were guarding. They attacked in full force and within four days occupied towns within a 200 mile radius of Mukden. The map shows that

The South Manchurian Railway where the trouble began: this photograph is supposed to show railway lines displaced by the Chinese

Chiang's message to the Chinese people

蔣總統告全國軍民書

「中國業已面臨一前所未有的重要關頭。日軍入侵我國領土，屠殺我國同胞，並損及我軍政當局之尊嚴。……」

47

this must have included territory far removed from the railway line itself. When the Chinese fought back the Japanese proceeded to occupy the whole of the province and drove the Chinese army out of Manchuria in a matter of months.

When the news burst General Chiang Kai-shek, the Chinese leader, issued the following message to the Chinese:

'An hour of unprecedented gravity has struck for the entire Chinese nation. . . . The Japanese army has invaded our territory, killed our citizens and inflicted indignities on our civilian and military authorities.

'The challenge thrown to us is also a challenge to all nations. The League of Nations was established to prevent war and bring collective action into play to stop aggression. We have immediately informed the League of the aggression and have asked it to obtain as a first step the immediate withdrawal of the invaders. The Council of the League is dealing with the matter at Geneva.'

A DIARY OF DELAY

On 19 September 1931 the Council met to consider the Chinese appeal for help. It was to be the first of many meetings which tried to find a way out of the problem which would be acceptable to both the Chinese and the Japanese. When pressed the Japanese representative appeared willing to co-operate. He declared that the only news that he had received was that his government had taken all possible steps to prevent the incident from leading to undesirable complications.

At the meeting of 30 September the Japanese accepted the Council's resolution which called for the withdrawal of Japanese troops to their original treaty positions along the railway line. But as October advanced it became apparent that no such withdrawal was taking place. In fact the exact opposite was happening. To the world it seemed that the Japanese were deliberately deceiving the League. Today we know the truth was that the Japanese army was no longer controlled by the Japanese government. A war machine had gone into action with a mind of its own and neither the League nor the Japanese government could stop it.

It was December before the League came up with a constructive approach. Lord Lytton was to head a Commission to

FAR EAST CRISIS 3 WEEKS TO-DAY.

JAPAN AGAINST THE WORLD ?

A serious conflict between Japan and the League of Nations will come to a head three weeks to-day unless there is a change in the situation in Manchuria.

The League has decided that Japan must begin at once to withdraw her troops within the railway zone in Manchuria, and complete this withdrawal by November 16.

The League places upon the Chinese Government the responsibility for the safety of the lives and property of

---

IT MUSTN'T BE 1914 AGAIN!

FOR weeks past we have been trembling on the brink of another World War. The situation in the Far East is essentially the same as that of June-July, 1914. A shot fired in Serajevo then set the world in a blaze for four years, and to-day, eighteen years afterwards, every nation under the sun is still floundering in the wreckage of that vast conflagration.

Not one person in a thousand on that June day when the Archduke Ferdinand fell dead in the streets of Serajevo supposed that the matter had any concern for him. It was only another incident in the eternal Balkan squabble.

What did it matter to us whether the Serbian pigs were shut out by Austrian tariffs? We were so busy with our own domestic rebellion in Ulster that we did not give the incident a second thought.

But the match had been lit and the train fired, and in six weeks the world was engulfed in war.

Dangerous tension

In the same way, when Japan sent a punitive expedition to Manchuria last autumn, it seemed a matter of small account in the midst of so many more urgent troubles. Manchuria was hardly better known than Serajevo, and a local activities of civilisation cannot go forward.

Never has the world lived in such a state of nervous tension as that which afflicts it to-day. It is greater, far greater, even than that of 1914. Then we had not experienced and could not conceive what a World War would be like. To-day we know, and the knowledge adds to the terror.

Then, too, the nature of the clash when it came was known to us. We knew who would be against whom and for what we should fight. But in the chaos and disintegration of to-day no one can forecast where the blow will be struck, for what it will be struck, or who will be friends and who foes.

visit Manchuria and investigate on behalf of the League. The Commission was to consist of members from the five great powers: Britain, France, Germany, Italy and the United States. (The United States was not a member of the League but the Council invited a representative to participate: this was vigorously opposed by Japan.)

The months that followed were again punctuated by delays:

JANUARY 1932. In retaliation for an attack on several Japanese monks the Japanese military bombed Shanghai (far from Manchuria).

FEBRUARY 1932. The Japanese announced the creation of a new 'independent state of Manchukuo' in place of Manchuria. The new state was practically to be run by Japanese advisers.

MARCH 1932. A debate took place in the Assembly on Manchuria. It was decided to wait for the report of the Lytton Commission.

NOVEMBER 1932. The Lytton Report was submitted to the Council. It condemned the Japanese invasion and rejected the excuse that this was simply 'police operations'. It recommended that Japan and China should discuss the possibility of a separate state in Manchuria.

FEBRUARY 1933. The Assembly voted on the Lytton report. There were forty-four members present: forty-two accepted the report, one abstained (Siam), and Japan voted against it. The Japanese delegation left the Assembly.

MARCH 1933. The Japanese announced their intention to leave the League of Nations.

Nothing could be done by the League to prevent Japan's withdrawal. Nothing could be done to force the Japanese to accept the Report without resorting to war and the Assembly had carefully avoided any suggestion of this. The only consequence was that the League members did not recognize 'Manchukuo'—but that did not upset the Japanese. Thus the League was seen to be powerless when faced with the determined opposition of a great power. Japan had set an example which Hitler and Mussolini were to follow. Manchuria was the first stage in the League's downfall.

The Japanese
war machine
in action in
Mukden

Fire at the
Odeon:
Shanghai
suffers under
Japanese
attack

'The Doormat'. The Japanese were openly flouting the League and world opinion by their actions in China

Germany Withdraws from the League

Gustav Stresemann, German foreign minister 1923–29, had finally brought Germany into the League of Nations in 1926. This was universally regarded as a most important step forward. Stresemann himself had only gradually come to believe in the League as a genuine effort to preserve world peace, but from 1926 onwards he was a powerful influence for good at Geneva. He believed that Germany could and should work her way back to equality among the great powers by carrying out the terms of the Versailles Treaty, harsh though they were.

Stresemann died in 1929, and over the next four years the situation in Germany changed rapidly and for the worse. The world trade depression brought unemployment and misery to all the industrial nations, and in such conditions extremists tend to thrive. In Germany the struggle between the political parties became intense and bitter, and it was finally settled when in 1932 Hitler's National Socialist Party gained more seats in the Reichstag than any other group. Hitler himself became Chancellor early in 1933. Once having gained power, the Nazis had no intention of ever giving it up.

17 Millionen!

17 million! The Nazis are voted into power, and their cartoonist celebrates

WE WILL HAVE ARMS AGAIN! 'WIR WOLLEN WIEDER WAFFEN'
For years Hitler had ranted about the injustice inflicted upon
Germany in the Treaty of Versailles. It was his declared aim
to tear up the 'shameful treaty' that denied Germany the right
to have a large army and to station troops along the banks of
the River Rhine.

'To what splendid use the Treaty of Versailles could be put.
Each one of the points of that Treaty could be branded into the
minds and hearts of the German people, until sixty million
men and women find their souls aflame with a feeling of rage
and shame, and a torrent of fire bursts forth as from a furnace,
and a will of steel is forged from it with the common cry: "We
will have arms again!"' (*Mein Kampf*).

The Nazi attitude to the League was quite different from
that of Stresemann. To Hitler, the League was simply the living
symbol and reminder of the hated Treaty of Versailles and

53

Germany's shame and humiliation. In 1933 notice was given
that Germany would withdraw from the League. Two years
later Hitler had finally repudiated the Treaty of Versailles
and commenced a full scale rearmament which was to lead to
conquest and war.

It is easy today to see that the German decision to leave the
League of Nations was a bad one—bad for Germany, for the
League and ultimately for the rest of the world. It was one of
the many steps which in a few short years were to bring the
world once again to war. We should try to understand how it
was that such a move was possible, and why, when they were
asked to vote for or against the action, most of the German
voters endorsed it.

The cartoon opposite is from the Nazi party's official newspaper, but probably a majority of Germans who saw it in 1933
would agree with the sentiment it expresses. Under the title
'Geneva's last chance' we are reminded that the allies'
promises to disarm, contained in the Versailles Treaty, had
not been carried out, whereas Germany had remained defence-
less since 1918. The French had a powerful army, the Germans
had a worthless promise. If the League could not put things
right then surely Germany must leave the League and make it
clear that she would no longer attempt to fulfil the treaty.

Genfs letzte Chance

Soll noch einmal brutale Gewalt vor verbrieftem Recht gehen?

'Peace (sadly): This looks very like the point we started from.' By 1929 the Disarmament Conference promised ten years earlier had still not taken place, despite endless preparation. It was in fact to be another three years before the nations could bring themselves to start disarmament talks

'The Conference excuses itself.' Despite the desire of the ordinary people of the world for peace the Great Powers were quite unable to agree . . . the Germans had walked out and were rearming; the Japanese were still in occupation of parts of China

A dove perched on a broken sword—hopes for the Disarmament Conference of 1932

THE GENEVA DISARMAMENT CONFERENCE

At the same time as they decided to leave the League, the Germans walked out of the Disarmament Conference which had been meeting at Geneva since January 1932. The Versailles Treaty had provided for it, and years of preparation had already been done before the delegates actually met. As they arrived at Geneva they were faced with the grim news that Shanghai was under heavy bombardment by the Japanese.

The Conference wrangled and talked for two years. Everyone agreed with the idea of disarmament, but no one would disarm. When the Germans walked out and the Japanese continued their attack on China the heart went out of the whole effort and the Conference broke up having achieved nothing. Far from reducing their armies and navies, the nations began to increase them yet more, each fearful of the future.

Italy Defies the League

THE WELL AT WAL WAL

Abyssinia is a dry and rugged land of rocky mountains and dusty deserts. In such an area the frontiers are often undetermined, mainly because of the difficult nature of the land. In November 1934 a Boundary Commission composed of Britons and Abyssinians was on a tour of the Abyssinian frontiers. The party, accompanied by some six hundred troops as a bodyguard against brigands, journeyed through the thirsty deserts of the region and on the 23rd of the month made their way to an oasis located at Wal Wal. The oasis was within the Abyssinian boundary.

To the astonishment of the party, when they arrived at the water hole they found Italian troops and a fort recently erected by the Italians. Angrily the commander of the Abyssinian troops confronted the Italians, and the British, sensing trouble, hurriedly left the scene. For several days the two armed bodies of men eyed each other suspiciously, refusing to recognize the others' rights to be there. Finally, in the blazing sun, shots were fired, and the Abyssinian commander fell dead. There followed a prolonged military action. Despite lack of heavy artillery the Abyssinian troops attempted to rush the Italian armoured cars, hoping, vainly, that they might overturn them. But with the support of aircraft the Italians beat them back and the Abyssinians were forced to retreat.

The news was flashed to the Abyssinian Emperor, Haile Selassie. He asked the Italians to send the dispute to arbitration so that it would be settled by neutral judges. Mussolini refused, and instead demanded compensation from the Abyssinians and insisted that they salute the Italian flag at Wal Wal. In the face of this insult the Abyssinians lodged a complaint against the Italians in the League of Nations. The incident at Wal Wal was to lead to an international crisis which finally exposed the clear inability of the League to protect small members when faced with the determination of one of the great powers.

THE LEAGUE AND ABYSSINIA

When Haile Selassie made his first appeal to the League in January 1935 it was proposed that independent arbitrators should be appointed to examine the incident at Wal Wal. But

Men of Ras Nasibu's Camel Corps. The Abyssinian army was ill-equipped to meet a European force like Mussolini's

Abyssinia and surrounding territories on the eve of the Italian invasion in 1935

Italian light tanks charging through obstacles

this took several months and in the meantime the Italians were pouring troops and materials into territory on Abyssinia's borders. It was clear that Mussolini was planning an attack. He had long dreamed of a colonial empire like those of Britain and France and the incident at Wal Wal gave him the opportunity to carry out his plans against Abyssinia. He did not expect any opposition from Britain or France who held adjoining territory, for they had often spoken critically of the fact that slavery still flourished in Abyssinia. Britain had actually opposed the entry of Abyssinia into the League in 1923.

Despite all the preparations that the Italians were making Haile Selassie still believed that the League would send some assistance if the attack came. Sir Samuel Hoare had declared to the League in September 1935: 'The League stands, and my country stands with it, . . . for the steady and collective resistance to acts of unprovoked aggression.' Such a statement from a British foreign minister was very encouraging to the threatened state. Action would have been more welcome still but this was not to be.

In October 1935 Mussolini launched the long-expected attack. Taking no chances he urged his generals to use the full arsenal of modern warfare. Tanks rumbled across the deserts and pounded mud huts and ancient stone buildings into fiery dust. Aircraft swooped down over the villages spraying them

The Abyssinian feudal levy assembled near Addis Ababa

with poison gas and inflicting hideous torture on women and children as well as soldiers.

The world reeled at the ruthlessness of the Italian attack. The League this time acted swiftly and Italy was branded as the aggressor by an overwhelming majority of the League members. A special committee was set up to study measures that members might take against Italy. For the first time in its history it seemed that the League was at last going to stand firm against an offending great power.

SANCTIONS: 'FALSE TEETH'

The special committee made the following recommendations to its members:

1. All members should forbid any loans to Italy.
2. Trade in war materials with Italy should cease.
3. Imports from Italy should be banned.

These were economic sanctions, and it was hoped that if they were employed effectively then Italy would be forced to abandon her campaign through lack of supplies. Unfortunately, although sanctions were voted for by League members they were never applied rigorously, and therefore this object was not achieved.

It is important to understand the attitudes of the British and French governments in considering why sanctions were not enforced as they should have been. Both were afraid of up-setting Mussolini. They saw in him a powerful ally against Hitler, whom they regarded as a more dangerous opponent. Thus coal and oil—the two most vital commodities of a modern war—were never included in the list of forbidden trade items. Both governments acted almost apologetically in applying sanctions, and a good many other League members never applied them at all.

THE HOARE-LAVAL PLAN: A SHADY DEAL

As the Italian campaign dragged on into the winter the French became concerned that Mussolini might turn on them and blame them for his difficulties. The British and French foreign ministers, Sir Samuel Hoare and Pierre Laval, drew up a secret plan. They arranged to offer nearly two thirds of Abyssinia to Mussolini if he would stop the war. The Abyssinians in return would be allowed access to the sea via British Somaliland. When the news of this plan leaked out to the British public, however, there was a storm of protest. It was seen as a betrayal of the Abyssinians and a gift for the 'bully' who had been branded as the aggressor by the League. Hoare was forced to resign and the plan was dropped. Such political hypocrisy by the major powers of the League was most distressing to Haile Selassie. Clearly the League was being sabotaged from within.

The effects of half-hearted sanctions on the Italians were the opposite to what had been intended. A visitor to Italy at the time would have been struck by the popularity of the war and the universal enthusiasm for Mussolini. Italians were furious with the League. It seemed that it was being used to prevent them from having colonies like those of Britain and France. They saw Abyssinia as a barbaric country which they would civilize. Angrily they declared that they would boycott the goods of any country that operated sanctions against them. Wives and mothers queued up to hand in their gold wedding rings to be melted down for the war effort. In return they received a steel ring inscribed 'Gold For the Fatherland'. Half-hearted sanctions therefore rallied the Italians around their leader and gave him the support that otherwise he might not have had. In triumph the Italians learned of their victory over the Abyssinians in May 1936. Their cheers reflected more than

Tearing up the tram lines in Rome. Sanctions caused a temporary scarcity of metal

An acid comment on events in Abyssinia

Barbarism   Civilization

63

a victory over the Abyssinians, however, They were also cheers for the defeat of the League in its attempts to prevent their colonial war.

HAILE SELASSIE ADDRESSES THE LEAGUE

The victory of Mussolini was the death blow for the League of Nations as a peace-keeping body. It was quite clear that when the great powers wanted their way they were prepared to ignore the League. The Japanese had ignored the League over Manchuria and Mussolini had done the same over Abyssinia. The Hoare-Laval Plan during the Abyssinian war revealed that the British and the French also were prepared to ignore the League when it suited them. The outraged demonstrations of the British public over this plan were of no use to small powers like Abyssinia. Action was needed, not words. Economic sanctions were no substitute for determined, joint action against the aggressor. Peace would not come through wishing for it.

When it was proposed to remove the ineffective sanctions Haile Selassie himself came to address the Assembly:

'I, Haile Selassie, Emperor of Abyssinia, am here today to claim that justice which is due to my people and the assistance promised to it eight months ago when fifty nations asserted that aggression had been committed. . . . I assert that the problem submitted to the Assembly today is a much wider one than the removal of sanctions. It is not merely a settlement of Italian aggression. It is the very existence of the League of Nations . . . it is the value of promises made to small States that their integrity and independence be respected and ensured. God and history will remember your judgments. . . . Does this mean in practice the abandonment of Abyssinia to her aggressor? Representatives of the world, I have come to Geneva to discharge . . . the most painful duties of a Head of State. What reply shall I take back to my people?'

It was a very emotional and telling speech. Haile Selassie's small figure confronting the Assembly was the equivalent of their consciences standing before them. Sir Anthony Eden describing the scene said of him that 'his was probably the only mind at rest. He had done all he could, and gazed in quiet contempt at the hysterical Fascist journalists, hurling vulgar abuse, who had to be removed from the gallery.' (*Facing the*

64

The Emperor Haile Selassie addresses the League

'The man who took the lid off.' Mussolini had confronted the world once more with the problem of war

THE MAN WHO TOOK THE LID OFF.

Dictators, p. 388.) Later Haile Selassie was to say on many occasions: 'It is us today. It will be you tomorrow.' These were prophetic words. Hitler after this completely ignored the League in planning to strengthen Germany. He was soon joined in alliance by Mussolini, who withdrew from the League in 1937. After Abyssinia the League dropped right into the background and was ignored as a peace-keeping body.

The Duce looks down on Adowa. A monument to the Italian victory in Abyssinia

7 Failure

Europe Heads for War

During 1938 and 1939 Europe was shaken by crisis after crisis as Hitler pursued his boundless ambitions for Germany. Austria, Czechoslovakia, Memel (part of Lithuania) were all swallowed up into the new 'Greater Germany'. There was every sign that the German appetite was far from satisfied and that Poland's turn would come next.

Since 1936 Italy and Germany had been linked in the alliance known as the Rome-Berlin Axis, and the two dictators, Mussolini and Hitler, treated the League with contempt. The press and radio in the two countries poured on Geneva a stream of hatred and abuse.

The expansion of Hitler's Germany in 1938 and 1939

REARMAMENT: THE DEMOCRACIES ABANDON THE LEAGUE

Britain and France, faced with the menace of a Germany fully armed and bent on conquest, were spending tremendous sums in a frantic effort to build up their armed forces before war came. They abandoned the League Covenant and made no attempt to have the crisis of 1938 over Czechoslovakia discussed at Geneva. Smaller nations followed suit, and it was soon clear that most nations would no longer be ready to carry out the joint resistance to aggression that was the very basis of the Covenant. Only Litvinov, for Russia, stood firm to maintain the power of the League as it had been designed.

THE FINAL STEP TO DESTRUCTION

German forces attacked Poland on 1 September 1939. Perhaps Hitler had thought that Britain and France, having abandoned the Covenant, would let him go ahead without interference. But this time, thoroughly alarmed and determined at last to take the bitter action they had avoided on so many earlier occasions, Britain and France declared war. The world was plunged into six years of horror and misery, and the League of Nations, on which so many had pinned their hopes, was to most of the world just a memory.

The Second World War

The League, and the nations, had failed. From 1939 to 1945 they paid the bitter price of their failure.

After twenty-one years of uneasy peace the armies are on the move again, and Europe is plunged into horror and chaos. The 25th Panzer regiment at rest in a French valley

Growing up amid the destruction of war. Two children on the morning after an air raid. The picture seems to say: 'Surely mankind can do better than this?'

People of every colour and creed suffered equally the ravages of the war. Air raid damage in Singapore, December 1941

The Last Session
The Assembly of the League met for a final session in its old
home, the Palace of the Nations at Geneva, on 8 April 1946.
World War Two was over, and many of the delegates were
already active in work concerned with the new organization,
the United Nations. Some of the delegates remembered the
high hopes of the League's first meetings, twenty-six years
earlier. Among these was Lord Robert Cecil, who had helped
with the drafting of the Covenant in 1919, and who had even
resigned his seat in the House of Commons in 1927, in order to
work on publicity for the League. With many others, he had
seen his efforts for disarmament among the nations come to
nothing in the disastrous Second World War. It was a sad
occasion.

Over the next ten days the affairs of the League were wound
up. Sean Lester, the hard-working Irishman who had striven
to keep some of the League's work going during the difficult
war years, was made the third—and last—Secretary-General.
The Palace of the Nations and other League possessions, including all its archives and documents, were transferred to UNO.

Looking back, the delegates recognized where the League
had failed. Manchuria and Abyssinia had clearly been the
turning points.

'Yes, mon cher President, we know the World War began in
Manchuria fifteen years ago. We know . . . that we could
easily have stopped it if we had taken the sanctions against
Mussolini that were obviously required, if we had closed the
Suez Canal and stopped his oil.' Thus spoke the first British
delegate, Philip Noel-Baker.

SERVANTS OF A GREAT IDEA
The delegates knew that their work had not been all in vain,
for the League idea had already been reborn in UNO. 'From
now on,' said the president, 'we owe to the United Nations
all our loyalties and all our services.' His last words before
closing the session were these:

'We part as we have met, delegates of Governments, servants
of a great idea; and as we break up from the last meeting of the
League we all know that "its soul goes marching on".'

Left: destruction in Helsinki, Finland, caused by Russian attacks on the city

The League of Nations and UNO

Refugee Blues: W. H. AUDEN

Say this city has ten million souls
Some are living in mansions, some are living in holes:
Yet there's no place for us, my dear, yet there's no place for us.

Once we had a country and we thought it fair,
Look in the atlas and you'll find it there:
We cannot go there now, my dear, we cannot go there now.

In the village churchyard there grows an old yew,
Every spring it blossoms anew:
Old passports can't do that, my dear, old passports can't do that.

The consul banged the table and said;
'If you've got no passport you're officially dead':
But we are still alive, my dear, but we are still alive.

Went to a committee; they offered me a chair;
Asked me politely to return next year:
But where shall we go today, my dear, but where shall we go today?

Came to a public meeting; the speaker got up and said:
'If we let them in, they will steal our daily bread';
He was talking of you and me, my dear, he was talking of you and me.

Thought I heard the thunder rumbling in the sky;
It was Hitler over Europe, saying: 'They must die';
O we were in his mind, my dear, O we were in his mind.

Saw a poodle in a jacket fastened with a pin,
Saw a door opened and a cat let in: [Jews.
But they weren't German Jews, my dear, but they weren't German

Went down the harbour and stood upon the quay,
Saw the fish swimming as if they were free:
Only ten feet away, my dear, only ten feet away.

Failure

Walked through a wood, saw the birds in the trees;
They had no politicians and sang at their ease:
They weren't the human race, my dear, they weren't the human race.

Dreamed I saw a building with a thousand floors,
A thousand windows and a thousand doors;
Not one of them was ours, my dear, not one of them was ours.

Stood on a great plain in the falling snow;
Ten thousand soldiers marched to and fro:
Looking for you and me, my dear, looking for you and me.

8 The Birth of UNO

A Deadly Mission

6 August 1945

0245	take-off
0300	started final loading of gun
0315	finished loading
0730	red plugs in
0741	started climb.
0838	levelled off at 32,700 feet
0847	electronic fuses were tested and found to be O.K.
0909	target Hiroshima in sight
$0915\frac{1}{2}$	drop bomb

These extracts are from the log of a crew member of a United States special mission over Japan towards the end of the Second World War. It was a deadly mission. The task was to drop the world's first atomic bomb. No one knew what was likely to happen when it exploded. No one predicted accurately the magnitude of the force and destruction that were unleashed.

'First came heat. It lasted only an instant but was so intense that it melted roof tiles, fused the quartz crystals in granite blocks, charred the exposed sides of telephone poles for almost two miles, and incinerated nearby humans so thoroughly that nothing remained except their shadows, burned into asphalt or stone walls. . . .

'A printed page was exposed to the heat rays a mile and a half from the point of explosion, and the black letters were burned right out of the white paper. Hundreds of women learned a more personal lesson in the varying heat-absorption qualities of different colours when darker parts of their clothing burned out while lighter shades remained unscorched, leaving the skin underneath etched in precise detail with the flower patterns of their kimonos. . . .

'After the heat came the blast, sweeping outward from the fireball with the force of a five-hundred-mile-an-hour wind. . . .

The blast drove all before it. The stone columns flanking the entrance to the Shima Surgical Hospital ... were rammed straight down into the ground. Every hard object that was dislodged, every brick, every broken timber, every roof tile, became a potentially lethal missile. Every window ... was suddenly a shower of sharp glass splinters, driven with such speed and force that in hundreds of buildings they were deeply imbedded in walls—or in people. Many people were picking tiny shards of glass from their eyes for weeks afterward as a result of the shattering of their spectacles, or trying to wash out bits of sand and grit driven under their eyelids.

'Heat and blast together started and fed fires in thousands of places within a few seconds. . . . In some spots the ground itself seemed to spout fire, so numerous were the flickering little jets of flame spontaneously ignited by the radiant heat. . . . Between them, blast and fire destroyed every single building within an area of almost five square miles. . . .

Destruction in Hiroshima: the atomic bomb held fearful prospects for a divided world

'Thousands of people were simply fleeing, blindly and without an objective except to get out of the city. Some in the suburbs, seeing them come, thought at first they were Negroes, not Japanese, so blackened were their skins. The refugees could not explain what had burned them. "We saw the flash," they said, "and this is what happened."'

The number of people killed was over seventy thousand. Many thousands more died from their wounds. The deadly mission demonstrated that man had discovered an alarming and fearful weapon. The discovery underlined the great need for some kind of international organization dedicated to keeping the peace. Failure to make such an organization work might result in the destruction of the human race.

Looking Ahead during the Second World War

Long before the Second World War drew to an end the four great allied powers, confident of ultimate victory, had decided that a new international organization must be set up. The United States, the Soviet Union, the United Kingdom and China made this plain at an important meeting in Moscow in 1943.

The Great Powers had the backing of an enormous weight of world opinion. The terrible European War of 1939 had spread to Africa, Asia and the Pacific, and had underlined the vital need to tackle the basic human problem: keeping the peace.

During the next two years the details of the new organization were hammered out and agreed. This was not an easy process, for though the Allies were united in their resolve to defeat Germany and Japan, there were plenty of other subjects on which they were far from united. The goodwill born of wartime suffering and comradeship were sufficiently strong, however, for the obstacles to be overcome. In June 1945 fifty nations signed the charter of the new world organization, amid general relief and rejoicing.

Germany had been forced into an unconditional surrender the previous month, but Japan was still fighting vigorously. It seemed likely that the war would last for many months more, perhaps even for years. But six weeks after the signing of the charter of the United Nations Organization the war came to an

'And now let's learn to live together.'

77

abrupt and dramatic end. Two Japanese cities, Hiroshima and Nagasaki, were attacked by the new weapon of devastating power: the atomic bomb. The newspaper pictures which showed acres of rubble where only a few days earlier had been thriving cities seemed to spell out an appalling lesson for the whole of mankind: 'Solve the problem of war, or this is the fate that awaits you.'

Below are shown in detail the stages which led to the founding of UNO in 1945.

UNO is Born

1943 The 'Big Four' (USA, USSR, Britain and China) declared at the Moscow Conference that they intended to see a new international organization set up. The United Nations Relief and Rehabilitation Administration (UNRRA) was set up to deal with problems of medical care, food supplies and refugees.
A conference was held at Hot Springs, Virginia, USA, to discuss problems of food and agriculture.

1944 Meeting at Bretton Woods, USA, the United Nations set up an International Monetary Fund and International Bank.
Meeting at Chicago the United Nations set up an organization to control international civil aviation.
The Dumbarton Oaks Conference hammered out the main lines of the United Nations Organization.

1945 Roosevelt, Stalin and Churchill met at Yalta, in the Crimea. Further details of the new UNO were agreed, including the voting arrangements. The self-governing Dominions of the British Empire such as Canada and Australia were to have a separate vote each, as were the Ukraine and Byelorussia, two republics of the USSR. One nation, one vote, was agreed for everyone else.
The San Francisco Conference discussed the final form of the UN Charter. The Great Powers insisted on the right of veto so that any one of them could block a decision. The Charter was signed, and came into effect in October.

1946 In January, the General Assembly met for the first time, in London. The UN decided to make its permanent home in New York.

The Charter is born

Meeting Place of the World

The decision to locate the UN in New York was a reflection of the determination of its founders to move away from Europe and its age long history of conflict. North America represented the New World. Perhaps the spirit of the New World would affect the UN and make it more successful than the League in Geneva.

The site for the UN building was donated by wealthy American John D. Rockefeller, Jr. An international team of architects contributed to the new constructions. Soon a new skyscraper was nudging the shoulders of the New York skyline. It reflected in its construction and furnishing the many different cultures of the world.

Seven nickelplated doors contributed by Canada form the

The UN headquarters in New York

entrance to the General Assembly. The lobby has a statue of Zeus, King of Gods, donated by Greece; a Foucault Pendulum, a device which demonstrates the rotation of the earth, donated from the Netherlands; over all a life size model of a 'sputnik', donated by the Soviet Union. There are murals and furnishings from Norway, Denmark, Sweden and Brazil. An Inca ceremonial mantle three thousand years old was given by the government of Peru. Japan presented a Peace Bell, Yugoslavia an equestrian statue representing peace. Black pebbles picked up on the beaches of the Greek island of Rhodes decorated a fountain paid for by American schoolchildren.

The UN building became the symbol of co-operation and goodwill. Into its construction went the optimism of the whole world.

9 The UN Framework

How UNO is Organized

THE GENERAL ASSEMBLY

THE SECURITY COUNCIL

THE ECONOMIC AND SOCIAL COUNCIL

THE TRUSTEESHIP COUNCIL

 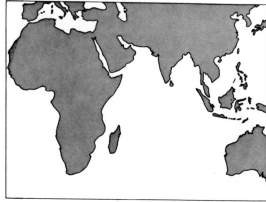

THE INTERNATIONAL COURT OF JUSTICE

THE SECRETARIAT

The General Assembly

The General Assembly is the main debating chamber of the UN. Almost any topic may be touched upon: water supplies, medical research, refugees, food supplies, border conflicts, etc.

Sometimes the Assembly may wish to make a recommendation to its members. If so, a resolution is proposed and voted upon. If two-thirds of the delegates vote in favour of it then it is adopted. All members have one vote each, although up to five delegates may represent one country. Adopted resolutions are only recommendations to members: they are not binding and sometimes members ignore them.

The Assembly assists the Security Council in electing members to other UN bodies: e.g. the Economic and Social Council, the Trusteeship Council, etc.

The Assembly elects the Secretary-General and votes on the admittance of new members, but acting on the recommendations of the Security Council.

The Assembly votes the Budget.

A debate in progress in the General Assembly. There are five official languages of the UN: Chinese, French, Russian, Spanish, English. Instant translations are provided by interpreters housed in glass booths above the chamber

The League of Nations and UNO
The Security Council

The Security Council now
consists of fifteen members.
Five of these are permanent.
The five permanent members
are the Great Powers:
Britain, France, United
States, Soviet Union, China.

After UNO was founded the Communists came to power in China
and drove the Nationalist government into exile on the island of
Formosa. Although the Communists controlled a population of
700 million compared with Formosa's 14 million, the permanent
seat in the Security Council remained in the hands of Nationalist
China till 1971. The Nationalists were then expelled from UNO and
the delegates from the communist People's Republic of China took
their place.

The non-permanent members are elected by the General Assembly.
Members involved in disputes under discussion may also attend the
Security Council meetings to present their points of view.

The main business of the Council is the prevention of conflict between
members. To recommend action there must be a majority in favour
which includes all five permanent members.

Any one of the permanent members may block action by vetoing it.
Abstaining from voting does not count as a veto.

In order to assist in keeping the peace the Security Council may be
summoned at any time of the day or night in the event of an emergency.
In the event of fighting between members the Security Council may
try the following courses.

It may order a ceasefire.

It may suggest to the parties ways of solving the causes of the conflict.

It may decide to impose economic sanctions against an aggressor.

It may decide to give military support against the aggressor.

But the Security Council cannot take any action if any of the five permanent members uses its veto. If one of these powers is involved in the dispute then deadlock will be likely in the Security Council. In this case the General Assembly can hold a special emergency meeting and consider the matter if it feels that peace is in danger. The General Assembly has been able to bypass the Security Council and the veto like this only since 1950.

The League of Nations and UNO
The Economic and Social Council

There are twenty-seven members elected by the General Assembly. Others may be invited to participate in debates without having any voting rights.

The Economic and Social Council supervises and works with a large number of subsidiary organizations and agencies. Between them they devote attention to the world's pressing economic and social problems. Topics debated include world trade, economic problems of under-developed countries, human rights, health, education and science. These are just a few of the subsidiary commissions and related special-ized agencies:

ECOSOC

COMMISSIONS	AGENCIES
Population Commission	Food and Agricultural Organization
Commission on Human Rights	World Health Organization
Economic Commission for Asia and the Far East	International Monetary Fund

The full list may be seen on the chart, p. 94.

The Trusteeship Council

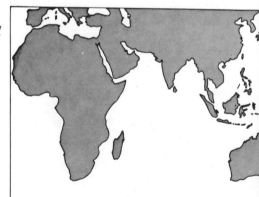

86

The Trusteeship Council *supervises* those powers who *administer* Trust Territories. These are non self-governing territories, usually colonies, that have voluntarily been placed under the supervision of the Council by the administering power. Some of the old League mandates were transferred to the UN.

The administering power has control over the day to day government of a trust territory. The Trusteeship Council receives an annual report on the progress of the territory towards independence. It may send its own observers to report on progress. The inhabitants of a trust territory may petition the Council if they have a grievance and the Council, if it feels that the petition is justified, may draw the attention of the administering power to it.

Members of the Trusteeship Council include those who administer trust territories, permanent members of the Security Council who do not administer them, and others elected by the General Assembly.

TRUST TERRITORY — ADMINISTERING POWER — U.N. TRUSTEESHIP COUNCIL

Keeping an eye on things: the Trusteeship Council supervises the progress of a trust territory which is dependent for its advance on an administering power

Examples of trust territories supervised by the Trusteeship Council:

Territory	Administering Power	Position 1967
Cameroons	France and Britain	Independent: Republic of Cameroon
New Guinea	Australia	Trust territory
Western Samoa	New Zealand	Independent
Tanganyika	United Kingdom	Independent: Tanzania

OTHER NON-SELF-GOVERNING TERRITORIES

There are some colonial territories that are not trust territories and are not supervised by the Trusteeship Council. A Special Committee was established by the General Assembly in 1961 to speed up the process by which these peoples would achieve their independence and freedom to govern themselves. There are twenty-four members and their task is to submit reports annually on the conditions and progress of these territories.

The League of Nations and UNO
The International Court of Justice

Fifteen judges are elected to serve the International Court of Justice, reflecting between them the world's different legal systems. The General Assembly and the Security Council vote independently for them.
Each judge must come from a different country.

The permanent location of the Court is The Hague, Holland.

The Court will give a decision where disputing parties request it.
The Court will also give advice or guidance to the Assembly or Council upon request, and performs the task of interpreting international treaties and conventions.
Decisions must be based on a majority of those judges present, and at least nine must be present. Reasons for the decision are published.

Any judge is entitled to publish his reasons if he disagrees with the majority verdict.

The Secretariat

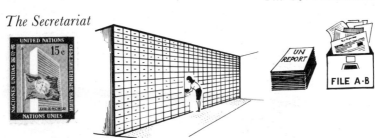

The Secretariat is the international civil service of UNO, carrying the burden of administration.

It has the vital task of providing information, preparing reports and keeping records for the Assembly and the Security Council.

Scientists   Librarians   Accountants   Lawyers   Artists

Typists   Broadcasters   Surveyors   Technicians   Interpreters

Some of the specialists employed in the Secretariat are shown above. There are over 6,000 staff members and 3,600 of these work at the UN building in New York.

The Secretary-General

The chief administrative officer of UNO is the Secretary-General. He is appointed by the General Assembly on a majority vote. He is recommended to the General Assembly by the Security Council where all the permanent members must agree on the nomination. At any time the Secretary-General may draw the attention of the Security Council to a problem affecting the peace of the world. From time to time he may undertake a special mission on behalf of any of the organs of UNO. Each year he submits the budget to the General Assembly. Each year he makes a report to the Assembly on the running of the whole organization.

The first Secretary-General was Trygve Lie, a Norwegian. His task was to steer the UN through the difficult days following the end of the Second World War. He was a determined man but although he worked hard for international understanding he found himself up against very

Servants of the world: *left*: Trygve Lie of Norway, first Secretary-General 1946–1952, *centre*: Dag Hammarskjöld of Sweden, 1953–1961, *right*: U Thant of Burma, 1962–1971

difficult problems. The 'cold war' developed between the USA and the USSR, and the Russians became very unco-operative in the UN. During the Korean War, 1950–52, they accused him of favouring the western nations as opposed to communist nations. Following his retirement there was difficulty in finding someone to succeed him who was acceptable to all the great powers.

Eventually Dag Hammarskjöld of Sweden was elected as Trygve Lie's successor. Hammarskjöld took office at a time when the Secretary-General's position was under heavy criticism, especially from the Russians. In the background of the 'cold war' it seemed that whoever acted as Secretary-General was liable to be accused by one side or the other of favouritism. Nevertheless, he set about his duties determined to resist all such accusations. He saw himself as an international civil servant with no loyalties but to the UN. He cultivated few close friends and was noted for his austerity. He worked excessively long hours and was ready to go wherever the UN directed him in the interests of preserving peace.

It was on a peace-keeping mission that Hammarskjöld died, in an air crash in the Congo, 1961. The eruption of violence had caused considerable animosity between the great powers. The Russians declared that the UN should not interfere in the Congo since the disturbances were internal affairs of no concern to outsiders. Although they had supported the original decision to send a peace-keeping force they changed their minds as the violence continued, insisting that the presence of UN troops contributed to the violence. Despite the criticisms levelled at him by the Russians, and indeed by other nations, Hammarskjöld remained determined that the UN peace-keeping forces should stay in the Congo until directed by the General Assembly to withdraw. He painstakingly emphasized that the UN troops were neutral in the internal struggle in the Congo and their orders were to protect people of all races and to fight only in self-defence. As UN troops became more and more embroiled in fighting he flew out to discuss peace with the rebel Congolese and it was on this mission that he died.

Hammarskjöld's death was a blow to the UN. Despite the controversy over his actions in the Congo many people had recognized his sincerity as an international civil servant. He appeared to have made the office of Secretary-General one of the most important organs of the UN. His death once again raised difficulties about finding a successor.

Alarmed by the violence surrounding the UN peace-keeping forces in the Congo the Russians pressed a proposal which they had made several times before. They suggested that the single Secretary-General should be replaced by three men acting together: a 'troika'. One man would represent the western powers, one man the communist powers, and the third the neutral countries. Since each would have a veto it would be possible to block controversial proposals like the Congo peace-keeping operation.

The troika reform was vigorously opposed by many members of the UN. It seemed to break the very principles upon which the UN stood : internationalism. It would divide the UN into power blocs and thus make it difficult to achieve co-operation. Each member of the troika would feel committed to the group of powers who nominated him instead of preserving neutrality and thinking in terms of loyalty to the UN. Since no agreement could be reached the troika proposal was not adopted. A new Secretary-General was elected from the neutral nations, U Thant of Burma. He was scrupulously fair and insisted that his secretariat members serve the UN and not their respective governments. Like Hammarskjold he worked unfailingly to preserve the peace of the world, travelling the globe on behalf of the UN. His quiet and sincere manner raised the whole status of the international civil service. It was from a suggestion of U Thant's, in 1969, that the idea of a UN university, dedicated to the study of 'pressing global problems of human survival, development and welfare' began to take shape in the 1970s.

U Thant retired at the end of 1971. Kurt Waldheim, son of an Austrian teacher, succeeded him. Waldheim had previously been Austrian Ambassador to Canada, and at first some regarded him as a colourless minor diplomat. But either they were badly wrong, or there is something about being Secretary-General which spurs men on to superhuman efforts, for Waldheim soon showed himself as tireless, active and shrewd as his predecessors.

(*Opposite*) From the Rio Grande to Cape Horn, every second coffin carried toward a grave contains the body of a child who has lived no longer than five years. According to custom, the young friends of the family carry the coffin of a dead child

10 UNO in Action

The Agencies and their Work for Mankind

Throughout the world UNO has come to influence the lives of many thousands of people through its agency work. The agencies are shewn overleaf. Their experts study problems in every continent, and their advice is given freely on a thousand subjects.

The UN agencies wage a continual war against unemployment, poverty, disease and ignorance. They are familiar with the terrible scourges of leprosy, yaws, sleeping sickness and trachoma—diseases hardly known to the richer nations of the west. They work to bring better standards of life to people kept on the brink of despair by crop failure, bad harvests or lack of water. They struggle against cattle and plant diseases which

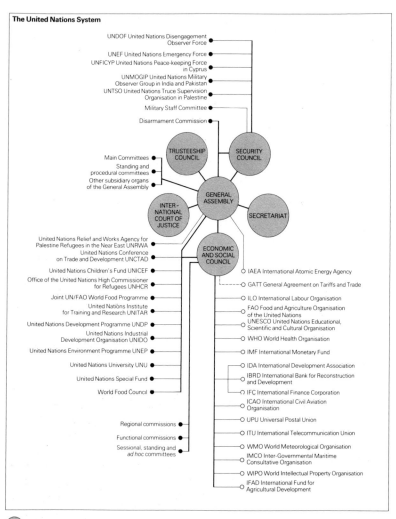

The United Nations System

UNDOF United Nations Disengagement Observer Force
UNEF United Nations Emergency Force
UNFICYP United Nations Peace-keeping Force in Cyprus
UNMOGIP United Nations Military Observer Group in India and Pakistan
UNTSO United Nations Truce Supervision Organisation in Palestine
Military Staff Committee
Disarmament Commission

TRUSTEESHIP COUNCIL
SECURITY COUNCIL
GENERAL ASSEMBLY
INTER-NATIONAL COURT OF JUSTICE
SECRETARIAT
ECONOMIC AND SOCIAL COUNCIL

Main Committees
Standing and procedural committees
Other subsidiary organs of the General Assembly

United Nations Relief and Works Agency for Palestine Refugees in the Near East UNRWA
United Nations Conference on Trade and Development UNCTAD
United Nations Children's Fund UNICEF
Office of the United Nations High Commissioner for Refugees UNHCR
Joint UN/FAO World Food Programme
United Nations Institute for Training and Research UNITAR
United Nations Development Programme UNDP
United Nations Industrial Development Organisation UNIDO
United Nations Environment Programme UNEP
United Nations University UNU
United Nations Special Fund
World Food Council

Regional commissions
Functional commissions
Sessional, standing and *ad hoc* committees

○ IAEA International Atomic Energy Agency
○ GATT General Agreement on Tariffs and Trade
○ ILO International Labour Organisation
○ FAO Food and Agriculture Organisation of the United Nations
○ UNESCO United Nations Educational, Scientific and Cultural Organisation
○ WHO World Health Organisation
○ IMF International Monetary Fund
○ IDA International Development Association
○ IBRD International Bank for Reconstruction and Development
○ IFC International Finance Corporation
○ ICAO International Civil Aviation Organisation
○ UPU Universal Postal Union
○ ITU International Telecommunication Union
○ WMO World Meteorological Organisation
○ IMCO Inter-Governmental Maritime Consultative Organisation
○ WIPO World Intellectual Property Organisation
○ IFAD International Fund for Agricultural Development

● principal organs of the United Nations

● other United Nations organs   ○ specialised agencies and other autonomous organisations within the system

can and do bring death to millions and the threat of starvation to millions more. Their doctors fight to save children from the early grave which is the fate of so many in the more backward countries, unless help is forthcoming. Their farming experts seek to make the land fertile, and to replace ancient, inadequate methods with more rewarding ones, often in the teeth of old prejudices and traditions which stand in the way of progress. They run camps to provide homes for the homeless, for the modern world with all its achievements has still failed to solve the problem of its refugees. The agencies are fighting in fact for human life, and for the chance for multitudes of people of varying colours and creeds, to live in safety and dignity.

The International Labour Organization

The ILO was formerly an agency of the League of Nations. It continues to study the conditions under which men and women work and live. Its experts devise and run schemes for training both workers and managers in countries where skills are in short supply. From time to time ILO produces codes or laws about workers in industry. It is hoped that the members of ILO—well over a hundred of them—will accept these codes and make them the basis for their own laws.

Workers' load limit — 121 lbs

Geneva, June 28

The International Labour conference today finally approved a recommendation that no worker should carry weights of more than 121 pounds.

The conference, the annual assembly of the 119-member International Labour Organisation, also gave its final approval to a convention on maximum weight.

The convention, binding on states which ratify it, states that no worker should be allowed to carry any weight likely to endanger his health or safety.— Reuter.

A typical example of an ILO convention, designed to help workers throughout the world

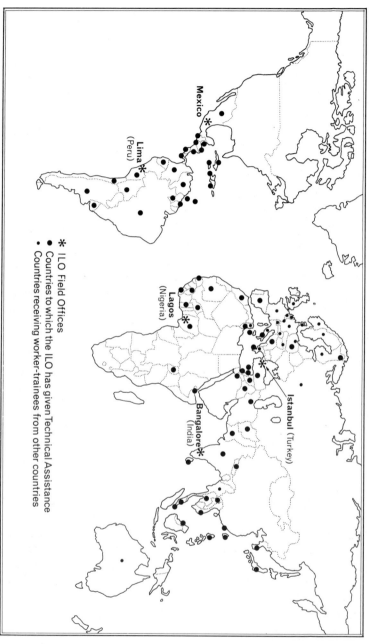

ILO's work throughout the world up to 1970

* ILO Field Offices
● Countries to which the ILO has given Technical Assistance
· Countries receiving worker-trainees from other countries

Mexico

Lima
(Peru)

Lagos
(Nigeria)

Bangalore
(India)

Istanbul (Turkey)

ILO watches and studies the effects of new inventions on workpeople, and has its experts who can advise how best to retrain workers who find themselves made redundant. Developing countries like India have had technical assistance to help establish new industries. Many countries, with ILO aid, have been able to start from scratch by teaching their people trades and skills which will help them to gain a higher standard of life. ILO work goes on in every continent, and students of many races are to be found at its two training centres, in Geneva and Turin.

WHERE THE BIRDS SING

Tzintzuntzan is a tiny Mexican pueblo on the banks of a lake. In the local dialect its musical name means simply 'where the birds sing'.

Many centuries ago Tzintzuntzan was the capital of a flourishing Indian kingdom. Then came poverty and decay and all that remained was a small community of potters. Their pottery was shoddy and fragile and the pots often broke before they could be got to market. There were no other crafts.

The highroad to Mexico City provided the only doubtful escape from poverty—migration. Tzintzuntzan's population shrank steadily until it could be counted in hundreds instead of the 40,000 of its heyday.

Then, some years ago, life began to stir again. The pueblo was selected as a good site for a handicrafts project and within a few months of each other two ILO experts moved in. The task of one of them was to improve the existing pottery industry, while the other was to introduce new handicrafts.

The potters liked to dig their clay alone, often making a hole which collapsed over them. Each year they had to go further into the mountains, bringing home the heavy sacks on their backs unless they could afford to buy a donkey. The clay was crushed by the women under big round stones. The pots were roughly made and baked in an inefficient home kiln. Then each one took his wares over hill and dale to market, where the pots, being frail and roughly made, fetched low prices.

The ILO expert had to show that clay could be dug more efficiently and safely and brought home in greater quantities if the potters worked together. There was good clay, far in the

97

mountains, which could be brought down by truck. Similarly, there were better methods of making pots and they could be baked better in a modern kiln. There were better colours and dyes.

While his colleague slowly won over the potters, the other ILO man looked round for new crafts to introduce.

There was wood in the forests if only the men would agree to build a road. Persuasion worked and the felling of trees began. A carpentry workshop was set up in the ruined palace of an Indian princess. Classes for the younger men were started. A good carpenter has some calculations to do and hence reading, writing, drawing, simple arithmetic and accounts had to be taught. The locals were not used to precision work. Why, they asked, should anyone want twelve chairs of exactly the same shape and size? They themselves had no furniture in their homes and would have been glad to have a chair or table no matter what its shape. The ILO expert knew that the introduction of new handicrafts would take time, but he was sure that artistic and creative instincts would assert themselves in the end.

The quality of the furniture began to improve. Motorists driving past on the road to Mexico City began to stop and take a look at it. Then, when its artistic quality was undeniable, motorists stopped, bought and took away the furniture in their cars. Orders came by post, and a small export trade began.

Other crafts have now been added to the new pottery and carpentry which have restored life and vigour to Tzintzuntzan. People from nearby pueblos come to learn the new and better ways of gaining a living. The ILO experts have left behind them an active, thriving community which is sharing its fortune with others.

Condensed from *Partners for Progress,* International Labour Organization.

The Food and Agricultural Organization

A wartime conference brought FAO into existence in 1943. At first it tackled the world's food problem by study and the spreading of useful information. Its activities and budget have grown, and since 1951 FAO experts have been working on every aspect of farming, fishing and forestry. Always the need is to produce more food, more cheaply, and in sufficient variety.

The Cedars of Lebanon: terracing the mountain slopes is an important part of the reafforestation work in which FAO is assisting

FAO experts concluded in 1963 that about half the world was hungry or ill-fed. By the end of the twentieth century food production would have to be trebled. The world's farmers, fruit growers, fishermen and foresters must make great changes if there was to be any hope of tackling the problem effectively.

CHANGES IN FOOD PRODUCTION IN FIVE CONTINENTS
FAO has proved that expert knowledge and advice can work wonders. With the Organization's help Cambodia and Mexico were able to increase egg and poultry production; the Panama shrimp industry was improved; and Egypt managed to double the amount of rice produced. A World Seed Campaign persuaded farmers to sow newer and better varieties of wheat and other cereals, with the startling result that the dramatic rise in harvest yields enabled some areas to export wheat instead of having to import it.

The World Health Organization

Since 1948 WHO has existed so the nations can unite to help one another in the fight against ill-health. Diseases cross national frontiers with ease, and it is to the advantage of all to

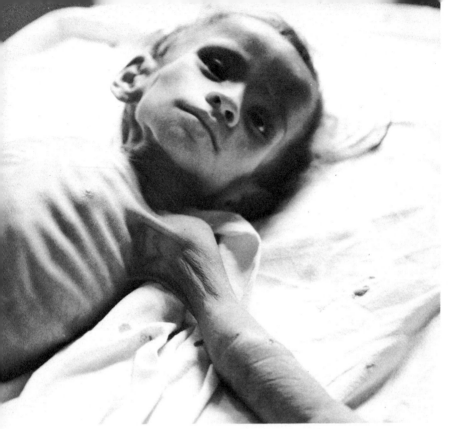

The scourge of malnutrition. A reasonable diet containing plenty of protein will restore this Peruvian boy to health. FAO is heavily involved in the problem of food production in South America, where there is much grinding poverty

El Salvador, where new fertilizers are in use as part of an FAO project. Local youth clubs have helped with the work, and here hold a musical field day

The Philippines, where the Ifugao people cultivate their rice terraces. They are no longer self sufficient, and FAO has helped with the work of improving yields

break the power of killers like typhus and cholera. WHO plans medical research, provides scientific equipment and trained staff, or simply helps with the cost of vital work.

COMMANDER IN CHIEF IN THE FIGHT AGAINST DISEASE
WHO fixes international standards: it makes agreements on the strength and purity of drugs and medicines throughout the world. As it also gathers reports, sends out information and assists research where it is necessary, it is very much in the position of a Commander-in-Chief in the fight against ill health who organizes the efforts of his various armies with a view to gaining a final victory. As there is a worldwide shortage of doctors and nurses, WHO runs numerous training courses, awards scholarships and does its best to promote health education. The problem of keeping folk healthy means teaching them to live sensibly, on a balanced diet and in clean surroundings.

A PROJECT ON CLEAN WATER

The importance of a good, pure water supply led WHO to set up a mammoth project to study the subject and take action wherever necessary. Over seventy nations have taken part.

Top left: UN experts study the water pollution problem in Europe: they are making a trip down the Rhine. Like many other rivers, especially those which flow through industrial areas, it is becoming increasingly impure. *Top right*: there is plenty of water easily available for these South Americans who dwell by the Amazon. But it is not always pure, and WHO must explain why it is necessary to go to trouble and expense in order to purify it. *Bottom left*: water is vital for cleanliness as well as for nutrition. A Chilean mother takes her child to the stone bath. *Bottom right*: water by bullock cart, not by tap, in this remote part of Chile

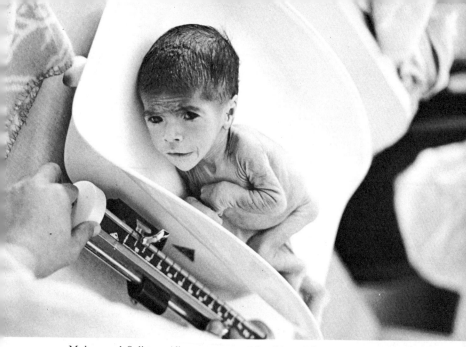

Muhammed Suliman Ali was seven months old, and fast approaching death. His mother brought him to UNRWA's centre in Rafah refugee camp in the Gaza Strip. He recovered after more than five months of treatment

Why do other people live in houses? These children at Bad Canstatt camp in Germany are among the one and a half million refugees who have now found a better life elsewhere, thanks to the goodwill of the Red Cross and other societies and the help of UNHCR

Work for Refugees

Two UN agencies tackle the world's refugee problems. They are: UNHCR, the Office of the High Commissioner for Refugees, and UNRWA, the Relief and Works Agency set up in 1949 to cope with the plight of the many Palestinian Arabs displaced by the bitter Arab-Israeli war of 1948–49.

Refugees are to be found in every continent except Antarctica. They are the pitiful by-product of wars, political and religious hatreds, racialism and intolerance. In some cases they have lived for years as 'minorities' among people of a different race or language, before being forced at last to flee.

POSTWAR REFUGEES IN THE CAMPS OF EUROPE

In the years after 1945 the refugee problem was mainly a European one, for armies had swept over the continent, frontiers had been altered and governments had in some cases changed radically and violently. Millions were displaced and homeless; the armies of the war years seemed to have given way to a new sort of army: the countless hordes of 'Displaced Persons', or 'DPs' as they were known. They faced a future which seemed hopeless.

As in 1919, however, help was on the way. Even before the charter of the UN had been signed the Allies had set up a 'Relief and Rehabilitation Administration'. Together with the Red Cross societies and others who wished to help, a start was made.

The chaos of postwar Europe made the task doubly difficult. Transport was dislocated and money was scarce. Many cities, particularly in Germany, were in ruins, with families living in cellars and bartering what possessions were left to them for food, coffee and cigarettes. 'Normal' life was far away for everyone.

The refugees were gathered together in camps, where medical care and education could be provided. The huge task of resettlement began. By 1951 over a million people had left the camps and found housing and work which enabled them to feel that they were ordinary human beings once more. Many had gone as emigrants to completely new surroundings where they could make a fresh start. Today, they are making their contribution to the life of the fast developing lands like Canada, Australia and the United States.

At school in the Gaza Strip: one of over four hundred schools run by UNRWA for Arab refugee children

The 'camp phase' of refugee work ended in Europe in the fifties. Since then the UN agencies have had to meet new refugee problems as they have arisen, sometimes very suddenly.

REFUGEE EMERGENCIES THROUGHOUT THE WORLD

No sooner was one refugee problem solved than another appeared, and this has continued to be the pattern since 1948. In that year the sudden emergence of the state of Israel on the map of the middle East sent over a million Arabs fleeing from their homes (see Chapter 12). The UN acted promptly and established its Relief and Works Agency, calling on help from

Refugees of 1967 crossing the ruined Allenby bridge over the river Jordan. Some of them have fled from their homes twice in eleven years

every quarter. UNRWA set up camps, schools, medical centres and points from which food was given out. UNRWA was intended as a temporary agency, but the problem continues, made worse by further Arab-Israeli wars.

In 1956 there was a rising against the pro-Russian government of Hungary. It was rapidly suppressed by Russian troops, and over 200,000 people fled for asylum to Yugoslavia and Austria. The UN High Commissioner acted rapidly with support from many countries, mostly western. The story of the Refugee Camps set up after World War Two was repeated on a smaller scale, and Hungarian fugitives resettled or repatriated.

E

The size of the refugee problem in Africa and Asia in 1966

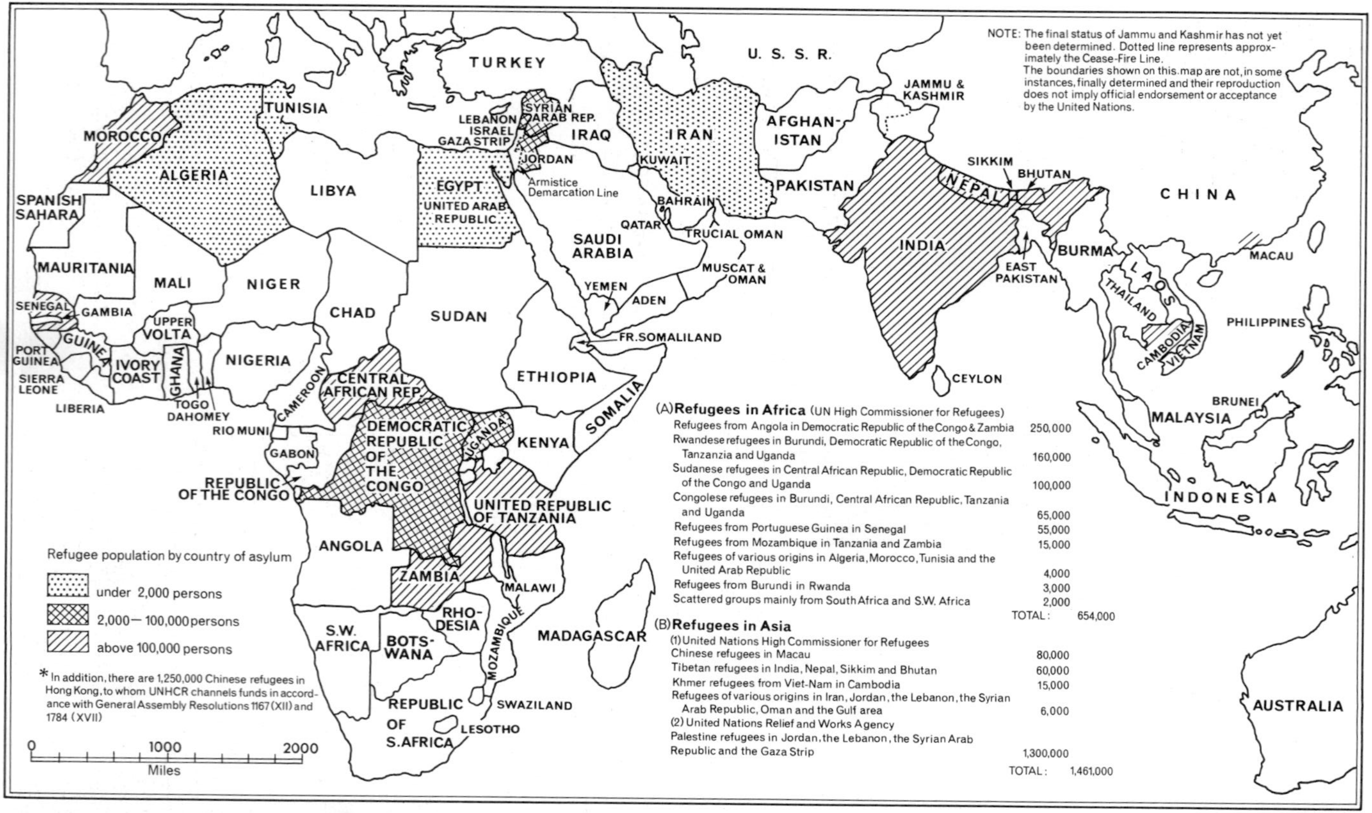

1959 was World Refugee Year, when an intensive attack was made on an appalling problem

The emergence of new, independent nations in Africa has inevitably produced fresh refugee problems. There were an estimated 600,000 refugees in Africa in 1966. Usually the urgent need in these cases is for food and help to tide the refugee families over until they can reap a harvest in their resettlement area. UNHCR has built up an extensive 'know how' over the years which enables it to do the best possible as the situations arise.

A LIFETIME OF WORK FOR REFUGEES

Typical of the many selfless people who work unceasingly for others was Madame Lucie Chevally. For fifty years she was active on behalf of displaced persons, mainly those arriving in France, though also much further afield.

At the end of the First World War she was in the Middle East, giving help to Armenian refugees. This was the time when Fridtjof Nansen was at his most active, and she met him in 1923. He urged her to continue her work, and the twenties and thirties saw her giving assistance to the numerous refugee groups who wished to settle in France. This continued through-out the difficult time of the German occupation during the

Left: Mme Lucie Chevally. After a lifetime of work for refugees, she was still active in 1965, at the age of eighty-three. *Right:* the Nansen Medal for outstanding service to refugees. It has been awarded since 1954

Second World War. In 1965 she received the Nansen Medal for her outstanding service to the cause of refugees.

Through the French voluntary society which she founded to help others, and in collaboration with the League of Nations and the UN, Mme Chevally gave a lifetime of service to the unfortunate and the homeless.

The United Nations Educational, Scientific and Cultural Organization
FIGHTING THE ENEMIES WITHIN THE HUMAN MIND

UNESCO is the Educational, Scientific and Cultural Organization which seeks to spread knowledge and bring the peoples of the world closer together in mutual respect, tolerance and goodwill.

Prejudice, racial hatreds and ignorance of the other peoples of the world are the deadly enemies of progress. Yet only about half of the world's children go to school, and fewer still carry their education beyond the primary stage. It is problems like this with which UNESCO must grapple, seeking to advise member governments how best to banish illiteracy and ignorance.

UNESCO gives scholarships for travel and study, and publishes hundreds of books and pamphlets in the main UN languages. To spread information like this is also to spread understanding.

SOME MAJOR UNESCO PROJECTS

1. *Adult education:* how it can be extended in various areas; methods which can be used to teach adults, especially to read and write..

2. *The 'Arid Zone':* problems of the nations of North Africa, Southern Asia and the Middle East; plants of the arid zone; water supply, including the use of salt water; how living in this area affects human life.

3. *Mass media:* newspapers, television, film and radio. The growing effects of these in Africa and Asia; the effects of television and film on children and young people; the use of the mass media in various fields of education.

4. *The different attitudes and cultures of eastern and western nations:* how we can obtain appreciation and understanding; the social position of women in the east; study and holidays abroad; the international exchange of books, works of art, etc.

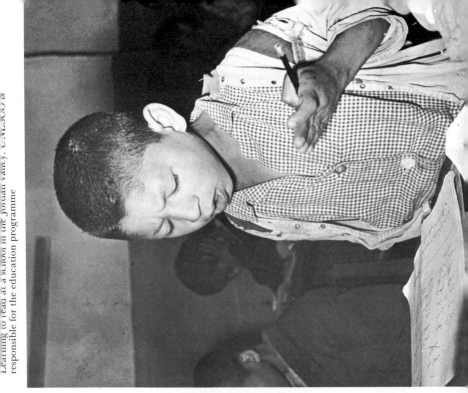

Learning to read at a school in the Jordan valley. UNESCO is responsible for the education programme

UNESCO helps in the running of UNRWA schools for Palestine refugees. A handicraft class in session

UNESCO is well in the forefront of the struggle for peace. Serving over a hundred countries on a shoestring budget its work has a tremendous potential value which cannot reasonably be measured.

Trade, Communication and Science

AGENCIES FOR INTERNATIONAL TRADE

One group of UN agencies is concerned with trade and commerce between nations, with the settlement of debts, and the tariffs which countries place on imports from other lands. The earliest of these agencies, and probably the best known, were founded during the Second World War by an international conference which met in 1944 at Bretton Woods, in the USA. They are the International Bank for Reconstruction and Development, and the International Monetary Fund.

The Bank's work is explained by its title, and it has loaned money for important projects all over the world. Often the loan is for schemes like road or railway building, for dams, or for hydroelectric plant to produce cheap electricity. The Fund deals with the world's many different currencies, and the way in which they can be exchanged for one another. It helps to keep them stable, so that international trade will not suffer.

An important trade agreement was signed by a number of trading countries in 1947: The General Agreement on Tariffs and Trade (GATT). It reflected the concern of nations to increase international trade by carefully revising tariffs which acted as obstacles to trade. Several GATT conferences have led to the reduction of thousands of tariffs on goods crossing frontiers. This has increased the flow of goods. GATT also supervises the trading relations of its members and ensures 'fair play' in trade dealings. GATT therefore complements the work of the UN agencies above concerned with international

trade and commerce. Today there are over 100 countries linked with GATT in some way, accounting between them for four-fifths of world trade.

COMMUNICATIONS AND TRAVEL AGENCIES
Increased contacts between nation and nation mean that a multitude of agreements have to be reached about postal arrangements, about shipping and aircraft services and movements, and so on. These matters are the concern of four UN agencies, dealing with civil aviation, the post, telecommunications and maritime organization.

MODERN SCIENCE AND THE UN—WHO WILL OWN THE MOON?
There is an urgent need for the nations to co-operate in the passing on and use of new scientific knowledge. The lessons learned in one country are often vital to all. The coming of the Space Age, too, has brought with it problems which UNO is helping to solve peacefully. The UN has therefore set up, as the need has arisen, a group of very specialized agencies and committees:

UN Scientific Advisory Committee
Scientific Committee on Effects of Atomic Radiation
Committee on the Peaceful Uses of Outer Space
International Atomic Energy Agency
World Meteorological Organization

ECAFE'S HIGHWAY ROUND HALF THE WORLD
UNO planners are accustomed to thinking on a grand scale. World problems can demand far-sighted, large scale solutions. A good example is the Asian Highway, commenced in 1958. A 34,000 mile network of roads is planned, linking Turkey with Indonesia and Java. Ferries are to cope with the sea crossings. Existing roads are being improved and new ones provided over some of the world's most difficult terrain. One of the routes involved building the world's highest tunnel, near Kabul in the heart of the Hindu Kush mountains. Sixteen countries are involved, and the final network should benefit 600 million people.
    ECAFE, the body which initiated this gigantic project, is the UN's Economic Commission for Asia and the Far East.

How do you travel—by car, camel or horse? A sign on the Asian Highway in Afghanistan, 1964. The World Bank assisted with the finance of this road

UNICEF Emblem

The United Nations International Children's Emergency Fund
UNICEF AND THE WORLD'S CHILDREN

The General Assembly was unanimous in setting up the UN's International Children's Emergency Fund in 1946. All nations, however they may differ on other matters, are concerned about the welfare of children and young people. UNICEF, now known simply as the UN Children's Fund, has thirty-three offices in various parts of the world. Its concern is with anything affecting the health and welfare of the young, and its brochures were able sadly to point out that in 1967 about 30,000 children still died each day of the year.

Drugs, vaccines, insecticides, milk powder, vitamins, soap, technical equipment such as drills, spades, vehicles: these are a few examples of UNICEF aid. It is a very incomplete list, however, and conceals much of the hard personal endeavour of those dedicated to the service of children everywhere. For example, there are nurses and midwives who make their rounds from village to village on UNICEF bicycles. UNICEF reported that in one recent year 6,000 bicycles were sent to more than twenty countries for this purpose.

UNICEF's budget is supplied entirely by gifts and the sale of small items like Christmas cards. A typical gift was reported in the UNICEF magazine for April 1967:

'The Halifax Tool Company of Yorkshire have donated a 14 HR Minor well drilling rig to UNICEF for their emergency programme to help the 60 million people in the famine and drought-stricken states of India.

'The Canadian Government has transported—without charge—four of the large Tiger mobile rigs, each weighing six tons, by huge Hercules transport planes of the Royal Canadian Air Force. They were flown from Manchester Airport where Manchester Corporation also waived all landing, navigation and handling fees. Air India transported the other seven small 14 HR rigs free of charge.'

Many schools operate their own fund-raising schemes on behalf of UNICEF. University Rag Days have raised money. All these contributions go towards the welfare of children and families throughout the world. It was very reassuring to learn that in 1966 the number of governments contributing to UNICEF was in fact greater than the number of UN members.

World Entertainers Work for UNO

Top left: Peter Ustinov, noted British actor and director, photographed at UN headquarters recording his part in a UNESCO-UN radio series. *Centre left*: Danny Kaye says 'Hello and how are you'—Thai style. *Bottom left*: Yul Brynner, another world-famous film star, looks out over a refugee camp in 1959 while filming *Mission to No Man's Land* for UNHCR. *Right*: All Star Festival: famous artists donated their talents to make this gramophone record in aid of world refugees. It was issued by UNHCR in 1963

There are many precedents for artists placing their talent at the service of a humanitarian cause. Yet never before have so many great names in the entertainment world been brought together. It needed the impulse of a world-wide endeavour. Out of the necessity to help refugees grew the idea of "All-Star Festival." The artists donated songs, some specially written and composed, others exclusively reserved for this record. The phonographic industry co-operated wholeheartedly and released their artists from their contractual obligations for this unique purpose. The trade has given its support. And so, thanks to the help of many, we can now present "All-Star Festival" as a great artistic achievement and a significant contribution to the needs of the refugees.

In the name of the Honorary Selection Panel, I thank all who so willingly responded.

Yul Brynner
Special Consultant to the High Commissioner
Chairman of the Honorary Selection Panel

Louis Armstrong

Maurice Chevalier

Lazy river (Carmichael/Aroud)
BING CROSBY and LOUIS ARMSTRONG
(By courtesy of Project Records)

The everlasting arms (Broones/Webster)
DORIS DAY
(By courtesy of Arwin Production Inc./Columbia Records)

Ximeroni (Hadjidakis)
NANA MOUSKOURI
(By courtesy of Fontana Records)

La vie est une belle fille (Willemetz/Kosma)
MAURICE CHEVALIER

First star I see tonight (Corso/Otis/Hendricks)
PATTI PAGE
(By courtesy of Mercury)

All of me (Simons/Marks)
ELLA FITZGERALD
(By courtesy of Metro Goldwyn Mayer)

Side 2:

Je m'imagine (Monnot/Raya)
EDITH PIAF
(By courtesy of Pathé-Marconi-Records)

When you belong to me (Cochran/Merrick)
NAT "KING" COLE
(By courtesy of Capitol)

Greensleeves (arr. Vaughan Williams)
ANNE SHELTON
(By courtesy of Philips Records)

Adonde vas, niño? (Don Porfirio Camar)
LUIS ALBERTO DEL PARANA
y su trio Los Paraguayos
(By courtesy of Philips)

Nobody but You, Lord (Jackson)
MAHALIA JACKSON
(By courtesy of Columbia Records)

La golondrin (Serradell/arr.Flor)
CATERINA VALENTE
(By courtesy of Teldec Telefunken – Decca Schallplatten)

Bing Crosby

Doris Day

Ella Fitzgerald

Mahalia Jackson

The League of Nations and UNO

' I Am the World's Surplus Man '

These lines were written by a Christian Aid supporter:

I am the world's surplus man.
Unnamed, unclassified, I appear as a marginal note
On United Nations reports,
A statistical stomach necessitating increased rice production
In areas hitherto devoted to mosquito reproduction.
I am anonymous, having no certificate of identity,
Appearing in no register of electors,
Though my family existed before Domesday,
Before Moses left Egypt.

I am a composite and cosmopolitan figure
—Jew, Arab, Korean, Malagasy
Too sick to work to feed my sickness
I paddle in malarial paddy-fields.
In long-house, shanty town or DP camp
I draw consumptive breath,
Consuming my loved ones in my own decease.
I breed
And though I give life I cannot give bread.
My son, wizened, stick-limbed,
Is one more decimal in the statistician's table.

My skin, bronzed to protect me from the scorching sun,
Is not proof against white man's scorn
(Though his chance of white parents was three to one against)
And the ambulance conveying him
To skill of knife and drugs passes me by,
Though my fallen-among-thieves body bleeds as blood red as his.

No tract or pamphlet finds a lodgement in my mind.
My met. report is written in stars and cloud formation,
My maps in track of man or beast.
I cannot mail my senator or write to my MP;
Inarticulate, I cannot communicate my joy, my grief, my pain.
I cannot appreciate
That the initials of UNO organizations form words,
Unicef, Unesco, Upu and Who.

Who, what, how, when?
When shall my need be met, my all consuming need
Which makes me less than man?
No-man, like Ulysses, a wanderer, un-certified, un-fed,
Treading this vast terrestrial globe
Like some caged rat in its mill.
What said your Lord?
'Feed my sheep'.   [brethren'.
'In as much as ye have done it unto one of the least of these my
How long, O Lord, how long . . .?

11 The Growth of UNO

A Worldwide Organization

UNO has grown with remarkable speed. The great majority of the world's states and peoples are represented. This is one striking difference between UNO and the League.

The antagonism between the Communist world, led by the Soviet Union, and the Western world, led by the United States, prevented any agreement being reached about the governments of three states: Germany, Korea and Vietnam. None of these was a member of UNO till 1973, when the two Germanys were admitted.

China: Communist and Nationalist

Civil war raged in China after 1945. The Chinese Nationalist government was eventually chased off the Chinese mainland in 1949, taking refuge on the island of Formosa. This government still claimed to represent the whole of China, and the

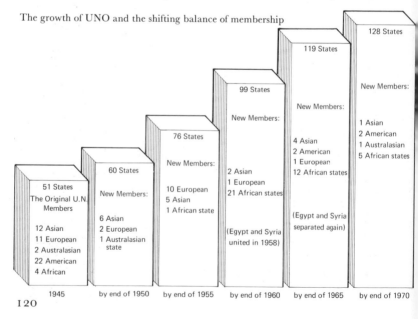

The growth of UNO and the shifting balance of membership

1945	by end of 1950	by end of 1955	by end of 1960	by end of 1965	by end of 1970
51 States	60 States	76 States	99 States	119 States	128 States
The Original U.N. Members	New Members:	New Members:	New Members:	New Members:	New Members:
12 Asian	6 Asian	10 European	2 Asian	4 Asian	1 Asian
11 European	2 European	5 Asian	1 European	2 American	2 American
2 Australasian	1 Australasian state	1 African state	21 African states	1 European	1 Australasian
22 American				12 African states	5 African states
4 African			(Egypt and Syria united in 1958)	(Egypt and Syria separated again)	

attempts of the Chinese Communist government to have the representation transferred to itself were always thwarted by the USA until 1971, when the Formosans were expelled and the Communist government admitted.

New Nations—by the Dozen!

In the 'fifties and 'sixties newly independent nations have emerged rapidly, particularly in Africa. Most of them were formerly parts of the colonial empires of Britain and France.

'I'm doing my best to get you in, pal.' Stalin's Russia tried again and again to have Communist China admitted to the UN. Although Britain and France had recognized the new government in China the USA remained determined not to do so. From The Herblock Book (Beacon Press, 1952)

They have tended to remain outside the eastern and western blocs in the UN, forming a third group. Ghana, Egypt and India have been active in leading this 'Afro-Asian' group. A resolution on the urgent need to end all forms of colonialism as soon as possible was passed unanimously in the General Assembly in 1960

It is unlikely that the numbers of UN members can rise very much further. Non-members at the present include one or two small states, such as Switzerland and Monaco.

The UN membership record is better than that of the League of Nations because its membership is far more broadly spread, and there are many fewer important gaps. So far there has been only one withdrawal: Indonesia, but this state reversed its decision after less than two years.

AGENCY MEMBERSHIP

It is not necessary to be a member of the UN itself in order to join the various agencies. Thus in 1965, although UN membership stood at 114, there were 126 members of the Universal Postal Union and 121 of the World Health Organization. Membership figures for some of the better-known agencies are given in the table.

UN and agency membership, 1969. There are some countries which do not belong to all the agencies. Britain, Canada and Australia belong to each one

Organization	Number of members
United Nations	126
International Atomic Energy Agency	99
International Labour Organization	119
Food and Agriculture Organization	117
United Nations Educational, Scientific and Cultural Organization	125
World Health Organization	128
International Bank for Reconstruction and Development	110
International Finance Corporation	90
International Development Association	102
International Monetary Fund	111
International Civil Aviation Organization	116
Universal Postal Union	138
International Telecommunication Union	135
World Meteorological Organization	130
Inter-Governmental Maritime Consultative Organization	67
General Agreement on Tariffs and Trade	76

12 Testing Time for UNO

Scores of problems have fallen within the scope of UNO since 1945. Wherever conflict has burst out efforts have been made to refer the matter to UNO for consideration. Some of these conflicts have presented UNO with the same difficulties that eventually destroyed the League. In this chapter four major crises have been selected to show how UNO has been tested and how it has survived where the League failed.

Korean Conflict

A TRAGIC DISCOVERY

Two soldiers seeking firewood investigate a devastated hovel.

'Inside it was dark, but a hole in the roof illuminated half of a large room, like a stable, littered with rice-straw, on which rested hundreds of empty ration tins, pillaged from the garbage heaps. There was a heavy sickly smell about the place which almost repelled them. . . .

'Cave had seen something stir under a mound of blankets in the corner. He went forward and lifted the corner of the top blanket while his nose twitched in disgust as the smell increased in intensity. He jerked off the blanket.

'Under it lay a boy of some twelve years, clad only in a shirt. His face was bloodless and emaciated; a death mask; but he was steadfastly licking out the inside of a ration tin, and continued to do so, though blinking up at the sudden influx of light.

'Cave's eyes followed the length of his thin, bare legs to the feet. One of them—the right foot, he noticed—was dyed a mottled black and purple, and the centre of it was open in a vivid crimson gash, oozing yellow pus.

'At last the boy dropped the tin and began to shake with sobbing, tears coursing over the tight skin of his cheeks through tributaries in the dirt worn by previous tears. . . .

'It was too appalling for words, and the reek of dead flesh was beginning to make them feel sick.

'They made their way outside again and hurried back to the lines for a stretcher.

'When they returned to carry the boy to the casualty reception centre a trio of others appeared, keeping a small distance apart. The departure of their companion broke through the protective barrier of their resistance. They stood around miserably in a small arc as he was loaded on, wailing in sympathy.' (From *Now Thrive the Armourers*, by Robert O. Holles, Harrap 1952.)

The incident described above shows the suffering that the Korean war brought to a twelve-year-old boy. Before the war ended some 60,000 boy orphans were to end up roaming the streets in search of lost parents.

A DIVIDED LAND

Korea is a peninsula lying on the east of the Asian land mass midway between China and Japan. For many centuries it had been fought over by these two countries. In 1910, however, it was attached to the Japanese empire. Thus with the Japanese defeat in the Second World War Korea fell to the victors.

The Americans and the Russians became the occupying forces in 1945. They divided the country into two zones of occupation, the North under the Russians, and the South under the Americans. The dividing line was the 38th Parallel. Their ultimate aim was to unite the country under one government. As relations between the United States and Russia deteriorated, however, this task proved very difficult. Co-operation between the two powers dwindled and finally ceased.

In 1947 the Americans brought the problem before the General Assembly. A plan was put forward for the holding of free elections and the withdrawal of the two occupying powers. A United Nations Commission was set up to see that this plan was carried out. Despite Russian objections the Commission commenced its work, confining its activities to South Korea. There, elections resulted in the establishment of the Republic of Korea with Dr Syngman Ree as its first President. In reply the Russians assisted the North Koreans in establishing a separate government for themselves and this was a communist government. Both the Americans and the Russians then withdrew leaving behind them a divided country. Each of the two

'History doesn't repeat itself.' This cartoon by Low reminded people of the fate of the League of Nations when it failed to resist aggression

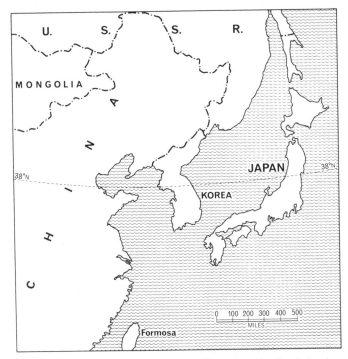

Korea: divided at the 38th Parallel. South Korea found itself an isolated tip of a peninsula menaced by the Communist governments of North Korea, China and the USSR

Korean governments regarded itself as the official government for the whole of Korea. Each regarded the other with growing suspicion and anger.

POWERFUL ENEMIES ON THE DOORSTEP

Events over the border in China made the problem worse from the point of view of the South Koreans. The Communists led by Mao Tse-tung drove Chiang Kai-shek off the Chinese mainland and seized power. The new government was warmly welcomed by the Russians who signed a treaty of friendship with the Chinese Communists in 1950. Thus South Korea remained an isolated tip of an enormous continent that was communist in government and hostile in attitude to the South Koreans. It was an uncomfortable position to be in, as events proved.

INVASION FROM THE NORTH

It was in June 1950 that the North Koreans invaded the South, striking for Seoul, the capital. The South Koreans were unable to resist the invaders and fled, leaving the capital to fall into North Korean hands. The very existence of the southern state was threatened.

For the UN this was a very important testing time. An attack had been made on a state which it had helped to create. It was a clear case of aggression. It was a situation similar to the Japanese invasion of Manchuria in 1931 and the Italian invasion of Abyssinia in 1935. Many people in 1950 could remember the last two situations and how the failure of the League to take strong action had ruined it as an international peace-keeping organization. Was the UN to go the same way so soon after its foundation?

This time, however, UNO had the backing of the United States which was most alarmed at the North Korean attack. The Americans had come to regard communism as their deadly enemy, fearing that communist governments intended overthrowing democratic governments everywhere. They were very hostile to the new government in China and constantly opposed Mao Tse-tung's efforts to join the UN. In their eyes Chiang Kai-shek on Formosa was the legal leader of China and his representative occupied a seat in the Security Council.

The North Korean invasion of the South was seen by the

Vital supplies from the United Nations for the South Koreans. The United States carried the heaviest burden of UNO's first war

Americans as a communist-inspired attempt to overthrow the democratic government established there. They were convinced that the Russians and the Chinese were supplying and equipping the North Koreans. They determined to act through UNO in assisting the South.

At its first meeting on Korea the Security Council met in the absence of Russia (which had withdrawn earlier in the year because the United States had vetoed the entry of Communist China to UNO). It called for an end to the fighting, and called upon the North Koreans to withdraw north of the 38th Parallel. Members were urged to 'render every assistance to the United Nations' in carrying out this request and 'to refrain from giving assistance to the North Korean authorities'. When it became apparent that the North Koreans were ignoring the Security Council call the Americans grew restless. The South was breaking up, everywhere the Communists were victorious. Finally, President Truman ordered the United States naval and air forces to go to the help of the hard-pressed South Koreans. At the same time he announced that the Americans would protect threatened Formosa from attack by the Chinese communists. The Security Council was informed that in offering military assistance to the South Koreans they were acting within the terms of the previous call to 'render every assistance to the United Nations'.

127

UNO AT WAR

A second meeting of the Security Council on 27 June led to the acceptance of the American action. This time members were called upon to give whatever assistance might be thought necessary to drive the North Koreans out of the South. During the next few weeks Australia, Belgium, Canada, France, the Netherlands, New Zealand, Turkey, the Union of South Africa, and the United Kingdom all sent military help to South Korea. UNO demonstrated for the first time that in the face of an aggressive war it would resort to arms in defence of the peace.

The intervention of the United Nations on the side of the South Koreans proved decisive. The North Koreans were forced to retreat and recrossed the 38th Parallel. Following up their successes the UN troops chased them even further north intending to unify the whole of Korea by gaining a complete victory. It seemed that a United Nations triumph was at hand.

CHINA VERSUS THE UN

In October the advance was dramatically halted. The Communists in China, witnessing the approach of American troops fighting their way into North Korea, feared for their own safety. They responded to this situation by sending massive military assistance to the North Koreans. The advance of the UN troops ground to a halt. Soon they were retreating. By the end of 1950 they had been chased by the Communists back over the 38th Parallel. The South was again invaded by the North, now with Chinese help.

This time Security Council action was blocked by the refusal of the Russians to agree to condemn China as an aggressor. The General Assembly considered the matter in December but members were very much divided. It was felt that the conflict was spreading and that the United Nations might be lending itself too readily to American complaints against the Chinese. Everyone knew of the hostility that had existed between the Americans and the Chinese since the Communist take-over. They had seen the Americans refuse the entry of Communist China into the United Nations. Some sympathized with Chinese fears of an American invasion, especially since President Truman had offered protection to Chiang Kai-shek on Formosa, far removed from Korea.

Daily Mail

FOR KING AND COMMONWEALTH

NO. 16,927 ONE PENNY ★ SATURDAY, AUGUST 19, 1950

INDIGESTION
Milk of Bismag and Stomach Powder

'AUSTRALIANS LAND IN KOREA'

4,000 are ashore near Seoul—Tokio report

Comment

AUGUST 19 1950

GIs ADVANCING ON 4 FRONTS	**Farouk: I will wed**
	Dead man left case

Daily Mirror

TUES JAN. 2 1951

FORWARD WITH THE PEOPLE

ONE PENNY

No. 14,662

Registered at G.P.O. as a Newspaper.

CHINESE HORDES TEAR BIG GAPS IN U.N. LINE, SURGE ON

THE second battle for South Korea has begun.

More than 200,000 Chinese and North Koreans attacked at dawn yesterday, and, surging over masses of their own dead, tore gaps several miles deep at a number of points along the 140-mile United Nations line defending South Korea.

The League of Nations and UNO

The effects of United Nations and Chinese interventions on the battle line in Korea

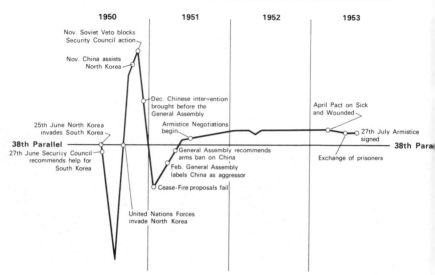

Eventually the General Assembly condemned the Chinese invasion of the South and labelled the Chinese as aggressors against the United Nations and the Koreans. The Chinese were slowly driven back but there was little prospect of a quick military victory for either side. Many feared that the war might spread, perhaps involving Russia on the side of the Chinese. When the American General MacArthur complained that he was prevented from bombing air bases in China by his orders their fears increased. While giving support to the military activities it had undertaken, the General Assembly also set about finding some means of ending the conflict by negotiation.

STALEMATE

The war lingered on for another two years with neither side making much headway. During all that time efforts were made to end the fighting. Agreements on the exchange of sick and wounded and on the exchange of prisoners preceded the actual armistice which was signed in July 1953. Korea remained divided with a frontier not very different from the 38th Parallel that had existed before the war started in 1950. All efforts to bring about unification since have failed.

130

A British officer, sten gun on his back, on location with South Korean soldiers

THE SIGNIFICANCE OF UN ACTION IN KOREA

The decision of the United Nations to send military assistance to a country that had been attacked by another was very important. It revealed that UNO, unlike the League of Nations before it, was prepared to enforce its decisions to the full extent of going to war. But in many respects the problem that arose in Korea had special features that made it possible for UNO to act.

For one thing, when the Security Council first discussed the matter the Soviet Union's representative was not present. Therefore, the one major power that had sympathies with the Communist government in North Korea was unable to exercise the veto. Then there was the fact that South Korea owed its existence to a UN decision, and in South Korea the UN Commission was able to report direct on the aggression from the North. Finally, there was the backing of the Americans who for their own purposes wished to check the spread of communism, and had the troops available with which to do it. (American troops were based on nearby Japan where they were the occupying power.)

Nevertheless the Korean War demonstrated that UNO was capable of collective action in the face of aggression. Although

Above: The aftermath of the Korean War: a boy refugee is rounded up on the streets. At the end of the war there were an estimated 60,000 boy orphans who were roaming the streets in search of their parents

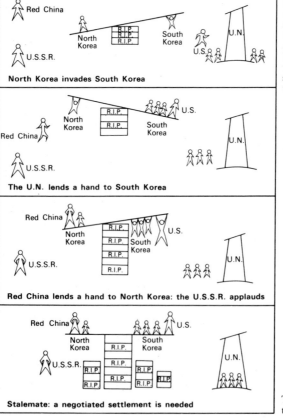

North Korea invades South Korea

Red China
North Korea
South Korea
U.S.S.R.
U.S.
U.N.

The U.N. lends a hand to South Korea

North Korea
Red China
South Korea
U.S.
U.S.S.R.
U.N.

Red China lends a hand to North Korea: the U.S.S.R. applauds

Red China
North Korea
South Korea
U.S.
U.S.S.R.
U.N.

Stalemate: a negotiated settlement is needed

Red China
North Korea
South Korea
U.S.
U.S.S.R.
U.N.

The balance scales of the Korean War

its action depended largely on the determination of one of the great powers at least it provided clear evidence that UNO, unlike the League of Nations, had teeth and could bite.

Israel and the Middle East

Since the days after the First World War, Britain had held the Palestine mandate. The land had been conquered from the Turks, and the Arabs who dwelt there looked forward to independence. But there were complications. Oil had been discovered in parts of the Middle East and so the area had taken on a new importance: especially for the powers of western Europe. There was also the growing problem of the Jews.

PALESTINE AND THE JEW

The land of Palestine held a peculiar and almost magical fascination for many Jews. Two thousand years earlier it had been a Jewish state, with a long history already behind it. Two unsuccessful revolts against Roman rule, the arrival of Arab conquerors and later the Ottoman Turks, had effectively destroyed any but the merest traces of its Jewish past. Nevertheless, the land still figured prominently in Jewish religion and hope.

JEWISH IMMIGRATION: THE ZIONISTS

From about the year 1900 a vigorous 'back to Palestine' movement grew up in Jewish circles. Some of these 'Zionist' Jews began to settle among the Arabs, though at first in very small numbers. Energetic and hard-working, they brought a sudden touch of the twentieth century to the age-old customs of Arab Palestine.

The British interest in Palestine and the Middle East was very strong. The Suez Canal had been a vital route for British commerce right from its opening, and in 1875 Prime Minister Disraeli had seized a sudden unexpected opportunity to buy for Britain almost half the Suez Canal Company's shares. In 1917 and 1918 British, Australian and New Zealand troops freed Palestine from Turkish rule, and the Arabs were led to expect independence by British promises. At the same time the Zionist Jews were excited by an official declaration that Britain favoured the setting up in Palestine of a 'Jewish National Home'. Either Arabs or Jews were going to be disappointed.

133

INTOLERANCE, HATRED AND MURDER

Small numbers of settlers had lived peacefully among the Arab population, but larger numbers of Jews arriving in the twenties and thirties caused friction. The trickle of entrants became a flood when the Nazis started their vicious persecution of the Jews after 1933, and violence between Arab and Jew became more and more common. Even 30,000 British troops found it impossible to prevent racial murder and disturbances which at times amounted to minor wars. The soldiers themselves were the target for extreme groups on both sides. The Palestine mandate was becoming intolerable.

UNO CREATES A JEWISH STATE

The obvious solution was to split the land into two. This was suggested in 1937 and again in 1947, this time by the UN. The UN plan was passed despite united Arab opposition, and the British thankfully prepared to withdraw, baffled and thwarted by the intense emotions which surrounded them.

ARAB-ISRAELI WAR, 1948

On the day before the British mandate ended the Jews proclaimed the existence of Israel as an independent state. War immediately broke out, with the Arabs attempting to destroy the newcomer.

Count Bernadotte of Sweden arrived in Palestine to work as a UN mediator for a peaceful settlement. He secured a ceasefire which proved to be shortlived. After months of incessant work he was suddenly and shamefully murdered by Jewish terrorists in Jerusalem. It was an end sadly in keeping with Palestine's record of violence and hatred.

An armistice was arranged by Bernadotte's successor, Dr Ralph Bunche, the distinguished American Negro who was to become famous as one of the UN's most devoted and hardworking servants. The Arabs insisted that it was only an armistice, and that they were still at war with Israel. The Israelis refused to tackle the problem of the many Arab refugees displaced from their homes, insisting that a proper peace must be signed first. The armistice proved to be an uneasy one, often broken by gun and rifle fire, duals between tanks or planes and 'commando' raids.

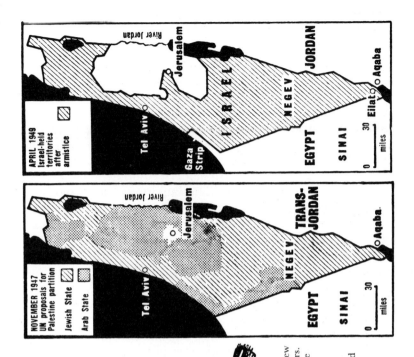

Above: 'Bloody punitive measures in the service of Zion'. A Nazi view of the British military presence in Palestine between the world wars. Zionism was the name given to the movement for the return of the Jews to Palestine

Centre: the UN's suggested solution to the Palestine problem: partition into Jewish and Arab states with Jerusalem kept as an international city. The plan was accepted by the Jews and rejected by the Arabs

Right: the state of Israel after the 1948 truce. The borders are merely ceasefire lines

World Crisis: Suez, 1956

EGYPT: AN OLD COUNTRY WITH A NEW LOOK

The smouldering hatreds of Arab and Jew, and the tangle of powerful western interests in the Middle East, combined to produce a world crisis in 1956. By this time Egypt's weak king had been deposed, and a new leader was in power. He was Colonel Abdel Nasser, and he was determined to build up the country's strength and influence in the Arab world.

New factories grew up, with modern equipment. Great irrigation schemes were started. The important cotton industry was encouraged and reached new heights of prosperity. The greatest Egyptian project, however, was the proposed Aswan High Dam on the river Nile, which would provide a wealth of electric power hitherto undreamed of. The World Bank, the United States and Britain had promised loans towards this gigantic undertaking.

While arrangements for the dam were going forward, Nasser pursued yet another project. For years British troops had been stationed in Egypt by a special treaty, and their main task was to keep secure the Suez Canal, one of the vital life lines of British commerce. But the Egyptians saw these troops differently, as an insult to their independence. They must go. Nasser negotiated with London for their removal. To the surprise of many Arabs, the British agreed, and in 1955 Egyptian forces took over the camps in the Canal Zone as the British army and RAF moved out. Egypt was jubilant, and Nasser's popularity had never been higher.

A WORLD WATERWAY IS NATIONALIZED

Suddenly the Egyptian success story received a sharp check. The World Bank and the western powers withdrew their offer of money for the Aswan Dam. Egyptian annoyance with the west knew no bounds, and Nasser replied with a dramatic move. The Suez Canal was nationalized, to become the property of the Egyptian people. Compensation was voted for the foreign shareholders.

It was a bold stroke, applauded by all the Arab countries. But in Britain and France the reaction was one of anxiety and suspicion. For them a vital artery of trade and commerce was in danger.

THE ANGLO-FRENCH INVASION

In October 1956 the Israelis attacked Egypt, claiming that this was the only way to stop the almost daily raids from the Egyptian sides of the armistice lines. Their armed forces swept all opposition before them as they raced south and west to the Suez Canal.

Immediately, the British and French warned both Egypt and Israel to withdraw all troops to a distance of ten miles from either side of the canal. Failing this, British and French forces would be sent in to secure the canal's safety. Twelve hours would be allowed for compliance. This ultimatum, and the invasion which followed, had been secretly planned with the Israelis beforehand.

There was no chance that Egypt would accept these terms, for this would have meant giving up still more Egyptian territory in addition to that occupied by the Israelis in their lightning strike across the desert.

An innocent victim of the Suez crisis: a young Egyptian boy, injured in a land mine explosion, is treated at a field hospital run by UNEF

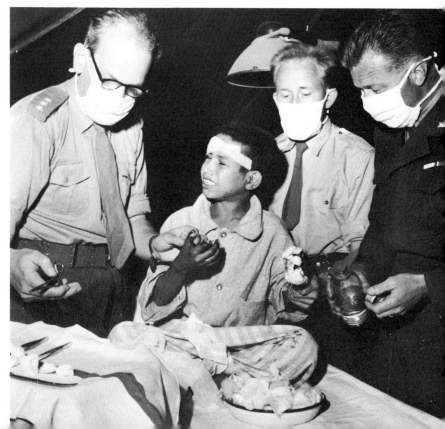

The Security Council was called into urgent session by the United States. Even as delegates condemned the British and French action the invasion fleets of the two powers neared the Port Said area. RAF Canberra bombers from Cyprus attacked Egyptian airfields; within a week the paratroops had gone down and the transports had landed soldiers. They found that the canal, undamaged during the Arab-Israeli fighting, had now been deliberately blocked by the Egyptians.

In New York the Security Council found itself completely powerless, for two of its members were in the very process of attacking a third state, without a declaration of war, contrary to international law and the United Nations Charter. The General Assembly took over, condemning the British and French action and demanding the immediate withdrawal from Egyptian soil of British, French and Israeli troops.

World opinion was overwhelmingly against the British-French action. From Russia came dire threats of nuclear attack on the two allies. The UN voting figures showed that Britain and France were isolated as never before. The peoples of both countries were completely divided and perplexed. The House of Commons saw some of the most disorderly scenes of its history as the Prime Minister, Sir Anthony Eden, faced angry MPs demanding to know whether the country was at war or not. In the face of such united opposition the two governments gave way and ordered a ceasefire.

A UN EMERGENCY ARMY

The Canadians proposed that a UN International Force be set up to deal with the emergency. Within a fortnight the first members of UNEF arrived in Egypt and the British and French prepared for evacuation. By Christmas their men had gone, their positions occupied by the blue-helmeted soldiers of the UN Emergency Force from Canada, Brazil, Finland, India and other states. It was another three months before the Israelis withdrew behind the old armistice lines and the crisis was finally over. UNEF remained to watch between Arab and Israeli, for the problem had not been solved: merely restored to the position before the fighting.

A STALEMATE, BUT NOT A SOLUTION

The departure of the invasion forces from the Canal Zone, and

UNITED NATIONS EMERGENCY FORCE

FORCE D'URGENCE DES NATIONS UNIES

قوة الطوارى ٠ التابعة للامم المتحدة

חיל או"ם לשעת חירום

No. _____ رقم ، מס .

This is to certify that the bearer, whose signature appears hereon, is a member of the United Nations Emergency Force.

Le soussigné certifie que le porteur de la présente carte, dont la signature figure ci-après, est membre de la Force d'urgence des Nations Unies.

Above: the identity pass of the international soldier, carried by all members of UNEF *Below:* blue helmets in Egypt. Canadian members of UNEF arriving from Italy. The Canadians were responsible for the UNEF resolution, and their soldiers were among the first to arrive in the danger zone

the arrival of UNEF, restored the area to a somewhat unsteady peace. Arabs and Jews still feared one another. Border raids were still common. The elimination of Israel was still the stated objective of six Arab states, and the Jews still refused to shoulder any responsibility for the pitiful hordes of Palestine refugee Arabs, making them a pawn in the bargaining for permanent frontiers.

NEW ARAB-ISRAELI WARS: 1967 AND 1973

Egyptian preparations for a new attack on Israel became obvious in 1967. Nasser asked for the withdrawal of UNEF, to clear the way for his offensive. But the Israelis struck first. They gained a lightning victory in the Six Day War which followed, occupying large tracts of Arab territory.

Six years later the Arabs launched a surprise assault on the Jewish festival of Yom Kippur, the Day of Atonement. Hundreds of Russian-built tanks rolled into Israeli-occupied Sinai; SAM missiles took a toll of Israeli jets. The Arab attacks were only mastered after ferocious battles. When a fragile ceasefire was agreed the UN sent another Emergency Force, Observers and Truce Supervisors to act as buffers in the dangerous No Man's Land between the armies.

The problem of the Middle East remains with us, and threatens to keep the whole area on the brink of disaster. The UN has something to its credit in the sensible partition plan of 1947, and in the work of UNEF. But the will to enforce the plan and the machinery to prevent war in the area have proved inadequate; the repeated Arab-Israeli wars have given clear warning that the tangle of hatreds and interests in the Middle East are a serious threat to world peace. The nations must find some permanent settlement, or pay the price. UNO may well have a vital part to play in this, but the initiative must come from its members.

Trouble in Central Africa

THE WORLD'S NEWEST REPUBLIC

In July 1960 the Congo was the world's newest sovereign state. Eighty years of Belgian rule had come to an end on Independence Day, 30 June. There had been speeches and official celebrations in the capital, Leopoldville. The people looked forward to a new and bright future.

Above: UNEF in the Gaza Strip: a perpetual Arab-Israeli trouble area. The street is decorated for the arrival of the UN troops

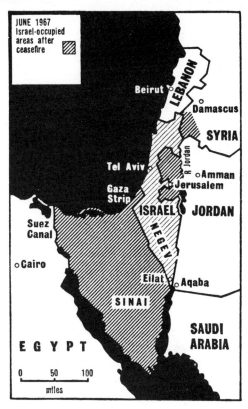

Right: Israel and the Arab states after the five-day war of June, 1967. The heavily shaded sections are the areas occupied by the Israelis

The optimism was soon shattered. The Congolese native army mutinied against its Belgian officers. Anti-Belgian riots broke out. White people were attacked, ill-treated and imprisoned, usually by native soldiers and policemen.

Reports of violence and a breakdown of law and order were so widespread that the Belgians reacted strongly. They flew in paratroops, often the toughest of soldiers. This was quite illegal, and resulted in an immediate upsurge of violence and rioting throughout the Congo. To make the chaos worse a native politician, Moise Tshombe, chose this difficult time to declare that the province of Katanga was no longer part of the Congo, but a separate state on its own. Within a fortnight of independence the Congo had been plunged into violence, confusion and uncertainty.

THE UN ACTS FAST

Patrice Lumumba, Prime Minister for only twelve days, and Joseph Kasavubu, Congo President, sent an urgent appeal for help to the UN. They were furious at the arrival of Belgian

The Congo, the enormous central African state in the service of which a UN Secretary-General was killed. Its area is about ten times that of the United Kingdom. The six provinces are shown

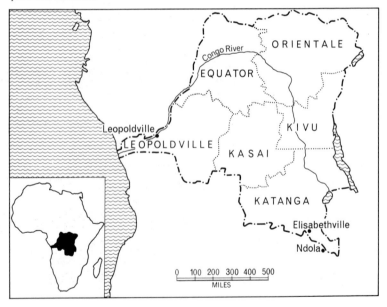

troops, and wanted them out immediately; they wanted technical help to set the new state properly on its feet; and they wanted the Katanga breakaway prevented.

The Security Council agreed to send military and technical help, though it did not make it absolutely clear just what the UN troops would be asked to do. Dag Hammarskjöld, Secretary-General, set to work and assembled a UN force. The arrangements were very complicated and meant contacting many nations by cable or telephone: yet the first UN soldiers flew into the Congo on the day after the Security Council resolution. The UN had proved that if only there could be agreement among its members it was capable of very rapid action indeed. The Belgian paratroops were withdrawn. Yet suddenly, the crisis worsened.

GOVERNMENT COLLAPSE
President Kasavubu and Prime Minister Lumumba quarrelled and in September 1960, when the President dismissed the Prime Minister, the latter retaliated by dismissing the President. Further complications were caused as army Colonel Mobutu tried to take over, forming a government of university students. Including Tshombe in Katanga, there were four separate groups in the Congo, each having an army of its own. The UN force was the only unifying factor in the country.

Daily Mail LATE EDITION

NO 20,007 (C) Associated Newspapers Ltd 1960 FOR QUEEN AND COMMONWEALTH FRIDAY, AUGUST 19, 1960

Canadians manhandled—then order goes out to airport troops: Shoot if necessary

CONGO THREAT to UN

Comment
FRIDAY, AUGUST 19, 1960
JARROW REVISITED
T HE wheel, as they say, has come full circle in Jarrow. This is the town

Dag warns 'Our job may become

Hooded train gang nail up the guard
THEY GRAB £8,000

THE UN NURSES A NATION TO STABILITY

The Congo had been ill-prepared for independence. Congolese doctors, lawyers, engineers and other professional people just did not exist. The UN, working from rooms in a hotel, set about the urgent task of running the country. A civil service had to be set up, hospitals reopened, communications restored. Suitable people, from wherever they could be found, were recruited to meet the emergency. At the same time, Congolese natives had to be taught to run their own country. The task that Belgium had so woefully neglected was undertaken by the UN. Courses were run to train teachers, engineers, civil servants, lawyers, police officers, air traffic controllers and other key personnel. Congolese were sent abroad on UN fellowships to study and fit themselves for eventual responsibility. UN experts were brought in—over a thousand of them—to teach the multitude of skills needed to run a nation. An impending famine in Kasai was staved off by prompt UN action.

A UN armoured car in action on the outskirts of Elizabethville, December 1961

A NEW GOVERNMENT AND A UNITED CONGO

Patrice Lumumba had been murdered during the turmoil and chaos of 1961 but gradually order returned to the disturbed Republic. The UN arranged for the calling of a new parliament, and in June 1961 it met, as conditions became more steady.

The problem of Katanga remained, for Tshombe still maintained its independence. UN forces moved into the province, but were reluctant to use force to end the break away. Belgian and other mercenary European soldiers assisted Tshombe in his defiance. Fighting broke out on several occasions. Dag Hammarskjöld, who had worked so hard for the Congo, was killed when his plane crashed on the way to meet Tshombe, at Ndola, in modern Zambia.

The continual attacks by Katangese on UN personnel, and Tshombe's unreliability, forced the UN to take firm action. The UN troops were involved in widespread skirmishing and sharp local fighting. Running short of money, and faced with

Canadians of the UN force restoring communications destroyed by Katangese troops

Indonesians of the UN force cross a river by means of a temporary bridge, January 1963

the united opposition of the UN and the new Congo government, Tshombe was at last forced to give in. Katanga was reunited with the rest of the country. The slow but essential work of building up the country could at last go forward peacefully. Although disturbances have occurred since, the Congo's debt to the UN is very considerable.

WHAT THE CONGO CRISIS HAD SHOWN
The obvious lesson of the Congo was that it was needful for a new nation to be carefully prepared for independence. Not only had there been a move towards civil war, but the danger of the conflict spreading to other nations was apparent to all.

For the UN, some interesting facts had emerged. At New York, the usual wrangling between Eastern and Western blocs had been overridden by the combined weight of the African countries. They had acted together and carried the great majority of the UN members with them. They were a force to be reckoned with in the General Assembly.

The UN had acted rapidly, too, thus answering critics who said it would always prove slow and ponderous. But the need for realistic instructions had also been shown, for the UN troops had been hampered by the order to use force only in self defence. How, for example, could they prevent the threatening intertribal warfare if they were bound by this order? And what about Katanga? Was this an internal matter, in which the UN ought not to interfere, or was Lumumba right in demanding rapid action against the breakaway province? Members were very divided over this issue and some refused to meet the cost of the Congo operations. Events settled some of these problems and eventually forced UN military action in Katanga. Perhaps delays in tackling problems might have been avoided by clearer briefing and more determined action from the moment UN troops arrived. However, a nation was rescued and helped back on the road to prosperity. A threat to world peace was dealt with through UNO.

Flare-up in Cyprus

INTERNAL PROBLEMS

It was just before Christmas in 1963 that the tiny island of Cyprus in the eastern Mediterranean erupted in violence. It was not for the first time. For centuries conflict had been a regular visitor. In the years following the Second World War,

Mediterranean trouble spot. Cyprus is only forty miles from Turkey but the Greek Cypriot majority on the island look to union with Greece some five hundred miles away

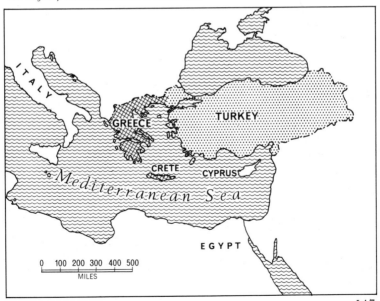

the conflict had taken the form of a colonial struggle for independence from the British. This violent and bitter campaign had ended in 1959 when the island became an independent member of the Commonwealth. But conflict did not cease when British rule ended. Other hatreds smouldered amongst the half million or so inhabitants and threatened to burst out into the open at any time.

The real problem is that Cyprus is an island of two races, two languages and two religions. About 80 per cent of the people speak Greek and practise Greek Orthodox Christianity as their religion. The remaining 20 per cent speak Turkish and practise the Muslim religion. These two communities viewed each other with intense intolerance. In the cities they separated and lived in different sectors. In the countryside villages were often completely of one race or the other.

Other factors combined to intensify the mutual suspicions of the two races. For centuries before the British arrival Cyprus had been governed by Turkey. The Turkish Cypriots looked for leadership to the Turkish government, only forty miles away on the nearby mainland. They declared that as the minority they were discriminated against by the Greek Cypriots. Rightly or wrongly they claimed that they did not get their share of the public purse. They wanted a partition of the island giving them complete self government in their part. These complaints were taken up and voiced by the Turkish government on their behalf.

The Greek Cypriots, on the other hand, rejected these complaints. For their part they looked for guidance from Greece. Indeed a strong movement had existed for some time which demanded union with Greece, even though Greece was some five hundred miles away. The Greek government supported this movement. Thus the island became disputed between the two mainland governments, Greece favouring the union, and Turkey favouring partition. Both sides adopted increasingly hard attitudes and the two island communities were encouraged to do the same. This was the situation that loomed when the British left and which finally erupted in 1963 when bitter inter-racial fighting broke out. It threatened to cause a war between Greece and Turkey which might itself become more widespread if other powers took sides.

Archbishop Makarios is depicted in this cartoon as following a policy calculated to bring disaster to the whole of the island

'Hah! We've given those Turkish Cypriots a nasty leak to worry about at their end of the boat'

RACIAL VIOLENCE

The conflict brought terror and disaster to the towns and villages. Armed raids were made by Greek Cypriots upon Turkish Cypriots, who retaliated. Public order broke down because Turkish police refused to co-operate with Greek police. Whole villages went up in flames and scores of innocent by-standers were killed during the racial frenzy. On the mainland the Greek and Turkish governments confronted each other and made military preparations to intervene in the island. They did have treaty rights to do this in the event of a threat to their security but their open intervention would undoubtedly lead to a full scale war between the two countries.

In an effort to smooth over relations between the two communities and to keep the peace Archbishop Makarios, President of the Cyprus Government and leader of the Greek Cypriots, agreed to allow British troops to return. But this measure proved unsuccessful. Memory of former British colonial rule was still too strong and the British troops once again found themselves targets of hostile demonstrations. Finally, in February 1964, Britain appealed to the Security Council and the problem was handed over to the UN.

UNO IN CYPRUS

The Security Council discussions resulted in a plan for a peace force to patrol the island. It was to be under strict control and had orders only to shoot in self defence. Its object was really to

149

Canadian UNFICYP soldiers on patrol in Cyprus

A UN soldier escorts an elderly Greek woman across the bridge from the Turkish sector to the Greek sector

operate as a buffer between the two races. In March 1964, under an Indian commander, Canadian, Danish, Finnish, Irish and Swedish troops flew in to join the hard pressed British troops already on the island. The United Nations Force in Cyprus, UNFICYP, was the name of the peace force.

UNFICYP did not find an easy situation. Each of the racial communities hoped that UNO would support their point of view. When it became clear that the peace force was steering a neutral course they adopted hostile attitudes to it and in some cases refused to co-operate with it. Undercover arming continued with support still coming from the Greek and Turkish governments. A clash in August 1964 resulted in 300 dead and several villages destroyed.

THE TURKS SEEK A SOLUTION BY FORCE

In 1974 the moderate government of Makarios was suddenly overthrown. Those who took power were extremists, dedicated to the idea of 'Enosis', complete union with Greece. The Turks reacted rapidly. On 20 July, four days after the coup, strong Turkish forces landed in northern Cyprus. They pushed rapidly inland, and by the middle of August occupied the northern third of the island. Not only was there civil war in Cyprus, but there was a real possibility of a Greek-Turkish war as well.

A truce was arranged. UNFICYP was reinforced till it numbered over 4,000 men. A number of its soldiers were wounded and a few killed as its units patrolled the 'Attila Line', the limit of Turkish advance.

The UN was powerless to stop the Turkish invasion. But the presence of UNFICYP, and the very existence of the UN, were both important factors in the situation. For one thing, both sides in the dispute used the General Assembly as a means of gaining support for their case. They were ready to talk and debate, and UNO provided the channel. The peace force was also able to undertake patrols at sensitive points and report incidents in a detached, unemotional way. Although a solution was not found the search for one continues, and when it comes the part played by UNO will have been significant.

The League of Nations and UNO

Your Attention Please: PETER PORTER
Your Attention Please—
The Polar Dew has just warned that
A nuclear rocket strike of
At least one thousand megatons
Has been launched by the enemy
Directly at our major cities.
This announcement will take
Two and a quarter minutes to make,
You therefore have a further
Eight and a quarter minutes
To comply with the shelter
Requirements published in the Civil
Defence Code—section Atomic Attack.
A specially shortened Mass
Will be broadcast at the end
Of this announcement—
Protestant and Jewish services
Will begin simultaneously—
Select your wavelength immediately
According to instructions
In the Defence Code. Do not
Take well-loved pets (including birds)
Into your shelter—they will consume
Fresh air. Leave the old and bed-
Ridden, you can do nothing for them.
Remember to press the sealing
Switch when everyone is in
The shelter. Set the radiation
Aerial, turn on the geiger barometer.
Turn off your Television now.
Turn off your radio immediately
The services end. At the same time
Secure the explosion plugs in the ears
Of each member of your family. Take
Down your plasma flasks. Give your children
The pills marked one and two
In the C.D. green container, then put
Them to bed. Do not break
The inside airlock seals until

152

The radiation All Clear shows
(Watch for the cuckoo in your
Perspex panel), or your District
Touring Doctor rings your bell.
If before this your air becomes
Exhausted or if any of your family
Is critically injured, administer
The capsule marked 'Valley Forge'
(Red pocket in No. 1 Survival kit)
For painless death. (Catholics
Will have been instructed by their priests
What to do in this eventuality.)
This announcement is ending. Our President
Has already given orders for
Massive retaliation—it will be
Decisive. Some of us may die.
Remember, statistically
It is not likely to be you.
All flags are flying fully dressed.
On Government buildings the sun is shining.
Death is the least we have to fear.
We are all in the hands of God.
Whatever happens happens by His will.
Now go quickly to your shelters.

13 Strengths and Weaknesses

An Historic Occasion

October 1960, New York: the city streets were especially busy with police car patrols. Time and time again the tall steel and concrete skyscrapers echoed the whining sirens. Snakelike, convoys of saloon cars glided swiftly towards the United Nations building towering over the East River.

Never before had there been such an impressive array of world statesmen assembling together in one place. The American President Eisenhower and the British Prime Minister, Harold Macmillan, were there. From Russia had come Mr Khrushchev, a vigorous and excitable leader whose promised speeches were awaited eagerly.

A score of other prominent statesmen took their places in the crowded General Assembly for the debates: Mr Nehru from India, President Nasser from Egypt, bearded Fidel Castro from Cuba, President Tito from Yugoslavia, Janos Kadar from Hungary, Nkrumah from Ghana in Africa, President Sukarno from Indonesia in the Far East. All looked forward to lively discussions, especially on disarmament.

They were not disappointed. Mr Khrushchev, small in build but forceful in character, proposed that all nuclear tests should cease and that complete disarmament should start immediately. The Americans and the British replied that they would agree to these proposals if the Russians would allow inspection parties inside Russia to see that they were carrying out their side of the bargain. Mr Khrushchev rejected this condition. To the astonishment of all present he set about attacking President Eisenhower and Mr Macmillan in a most energetic manner. From the rostrum he thundered at them, shook his fists, and at one stage actually took off his shoe and beat it on the table before him.

It soon became clear that no agreement was to be reached on the important problem of disarmament. But on the brighter

AND [ILLINGWORTH] COMMENTS

THE NON-U UN

New York, Sunday.

W HAT a roll - call when the Africans come marching in ! Like the throb of a slow drumb cat, this new roster : Cameroun . . . Chad . . . Dahomey . . . Gabon . . . Malagasy . . . Mali . . . Niger . . . Togo . . . Upper Volta.

The scene is the coming General Assembly of the United Nations. And these are the new members, the new nations spawned out of the immense dark of Africa.

Greet them with respect, for they are the masters now. They hold the balance of power of the new UN. They finally demolish the Old Club.

In this new non-U UN at last the majority deserts the West. Now it is a majority of the uncommitted, and on some scores like" colonialism," we astonishingly face a pro-Soviet majority.

We and the likes of us must get used to the odd idea that we are now a minority.

New-born African States come here to knock at the opening door of the United Nations eager young men grabbing in their proud but unpractised hands the reins of history, of power, of destiny.

by

STANLEY BURCH

think about it—the thought of what will happen when an army of this great army of negro delegates drives south of Washington . . . into the South, which is a white man's world.

The imminent humiliations shock the State Department's nerves.

Picture the lazy cross-roads of a small town in Georgia, in Alabama, in Louisiana.

"That crazy Niggra," mutters the cop, waving the motorist over to the kerb. He bawls at him about the red light, levels at him the contempt that has been levelled at the black man here ever since the white man raided Africa for his cheap labour.

side it was possible to look at the meeting in another way. The world's statesmen had gathered under one roof in a way never before seen on such a scale. The United Nations had presented itself as a useful meeting place where at least politicians were able to voice their criticisms of other powers. If shoe-banging was violent and showy it was an improvement on the old days of secret diplomacy when great powers nursed their suspicions in silence. Everything was out in the open in the General Assembly. The UN acted as the meeting place for the world.

UNO is Far from Perfect

Since the many new nations have joined UNO—over seventy since 1945—it has changed beyond all recognition. These new nations, many of them tiny and economically poor, may influence debates and decisions in a way never foreseen by the original founders. This is because a great deal of the decision making has shifted to the General Assembly in order to get round the constant threat of the veto in the Security Council. There, deadlocks often occur when the interests of the great powers conflict.

UNO has many weaknesses. The long exclusion of Communist China with its 700 million people was ridiculous. UNO could scarcely be described as a world organisation whilst one fifth of the world's population was denied membership. It was not until November 1971 that the communist People's Republic of China was able to take its seat in the Assembly and the Security Council. The suggestion that the Nationalists should continue as ordinary members of UNO was turned down at the same time, so it was the turn of the Formosans to be completely unrepresented at the UN. Their delegates were expelled.

The policy of 'one country—one vote' is also questionable. This puts tiny states with small populations on the same level as the great powers with their millions of peoples. These tiny countries are also often economically poor and heavily dependent on the UN for financial assistance. They contribute the least to UN operations and receive the most in aid. They are often critical of the great powers in the conduct of their policies. This has made some of the great powers lukewarm in their attitude to UN operations. Since they know that they may be outvoted by the new nations great powers often avoid raising

'What business is it of yours? Anyone would think you were world opinion.' UNO cannot interfere in the internal affairs of a country, as this cartoon by Low directed at South Africa indicates

UNO was powerless during the Arab–Israeli War, 1967, because both sides rejected UN approaches

their problems in UNO and adopt cynical attitudes to it.

Cynicism is one of UNO's enemies. There are some powers that urge UN operations against others but who ignore resolutions which prove inconvenient to themselves. Despite what the Charter says about the rights of individuals there are a number of dictatorships in UNO and their governments constantly ignore the Charter. Some members have refused to pay contributions when they have disagreed with the policy adopted. There are no penalties for dealing with these nations. They are still entitled to vote and speak in debates.

Because of these weaknesses the world's super powers, the USA and the USSR, have almost dropped UNO from their reckoning when they confront each other. In the Cuban crisis of 1962 when American and Russian rockets bristled at the ready UNO was ignored. 'Hot-lines', direct telephone links between the two major powers, almost ensure that UNO will take second place in a crisis between the great powers.

More talk, and still more talk. . .

There is, however, a very large credit side to this gloomy picture. For one thing the enormous humanitarian work of the UN and its agencies has done wonders in promoting international understanding. Genuine hardship and genuine need have been tackled on a scale that men had never seen before the existence of UNO. Men can unite for peaceful purposes and tackle nature's problems with zest and energy.

Again, although UNO has not always succeeded in preventing conflicts it has provided convenient channels for discussion and sometimes has dispatched a peace-keeping force. The UN building is a common meeting ground for its members. Without it suspicion of others would be nursed in ignorance. In the Assembly, and in the committee rooms, lounges and libraries of the UN building there is ample opportunity to dispel suspicions. Neutral delegates may often suggest solutions to disputing parties in these informal meeting places.

The achievement of the peace-keeping force for 'minor'

But it is better than allowing this to happen

World servants with a dangerous task

conflicts is also very important. 'Minor' wars are not 'minor' to those caught up in them. The peace-keeping force may also prevent a conflict from spreading and becoming a major war.

Compared with the whole span of human history the history of both the League of Nations and UNO is but a tiny drop in the ocean. Each organization has, however, provided machinery for keeping the peace in the short time of its existence. Failures may be traced to the unwillingness of nations to use that machinery. It is important, therefore, that UNO is not allowed to go the way of the League. Without a world organization the nations would slip back to the days of secret alliances and suspicions that erupted into the First World War. The more deadly weapons available for destruction make that kind of world a fearful place. Through UNO we must cling to the belief that it is better to talk than to fight.

'The shadow of the past falls across UNO'

LEAGUE
OF
NATIONS
Fell asleep
IN ABYSSINIA
AFTER PROLONGED
NON-IMPLEMENTATION
OF POLICY
ON SANCTIONS

Members of the UN with Dates of Entry

Afghanistan	1946	Democratic Yemen	1967
Albania	1955	Denmark	1945
Algeria	1962	Djibouti	1977
Angola	1976	Dominica	1978
Argentina	1945	Dominican Republic	1945
Australia	1945	Ecuador	1945
Austria	1955	Egypt	1945
Bahamas	1973	El Salvador	1945
Bahrian	1971	Equatorial Guinea	1968
Bangladesh	1974	Ethiopia	1945
Barbados	1966	Fiji	1970
Belgium	1945	Finland	1955
Benin	1960	France	1945
Bhutan	1971	Gabon	1960
Bolivia	1945	Gambia	1965
Botswana	1966	German Democratic	
Brazil	1945	Republic	1973
Bulgaria	1955	Germany, Federal	
Burma	1948	Republic of	1973
Burundi	1962	Ghana	1957
Byelorussian Soviet		Greece	1945
Socialist Republic	1945	Grenada	1974
Canada	1945	Guatemala	1945
Cape Verde	1975	Guinea	1958
Central African Empire	1960	Guinea-Bissau	1974
Chad	1960	Guyana	1966
Chile	1945	Haiti	1945
China	1945	Honduras	1945
Colombia	1945	Hungary	1955
Comoros	1975	Iceland	1946
Congo	1960	India	1945
Costa Rica	1945	Indonesia	1950
Cuba	1945	Iran	1945
Cyprus	1960	Iraq	1945
Czechoslovakia	1945	Ireland	1955
Democratic Kampuchea	1955	Israel	1949

Italy	1955	Romania	1955
Ivory Coast	1960	Rwanda	1962
Jamaica	1962	Samoa	1976
Japan	1956	Sao Tome and Principe	1975
Jordan	1955	Saudi Arabia	1945
Kenya	1963	Senegal	1960
Kuwait	1963	Seychelles	1976
Lao People's Democratic		Sierra Leone	1961
Republic	1955	Singapore	1965
Lebanon	1945	Solomon Islands	1978
Lesotho	1966	Somalia	1960
Liberia	1945	South Africa	1945
Libyan Arab Jamahiriya	1955	Spain	1955
Luxembourg	1945	Sri Lanka	1955
Madagascar	1960	Sudan	1956
Malawi	1964	Swaziland	1968
Malaysia	1957	Sweden	1946
Maldives	1965	Syrian Arab Republic	1945
Mali	1960	Thailand	1946
Malta	1964	Togo	1960
Mauritania	1961	Trinidad and Tobago	1962
Mauritius	1968	Tunisia	1956
Mexico	1945	Turkey	1945
Mongolia	1961	Uganda	1962
Morocco	1956	Ukrainian Soviet Socialist	
Mozambique	1975	Republic	1945
Nepal	1955	Union of Soviet	
Netherlands	1945	Socialist Republics	1945
New Zealand	1945	United Arab Emirates	1971
Nicaragua	1945	United Kingdom	1945
Niger	1960	United Republic of	
Nigeria	1960	Cameroon	1960
Norway	1945	United Republic of	
Oman	1971	Tanzania	1961
Pakistan	1947	United States of America	1945
Panama	1945	Upper Volta	1960
Papua New Guinea	1975	Uruguay	1945
Paraguay	1945	Venezuela	1945
Peru	1945	Vietnam	1977
Philippines	1945	Yemen	1947
Poland	1945	Yugoslavia	1945
Portugal	1955	Zaire	1960
Qatar	1971	Zambia	1964

Membership listed from UN information, August 1979.

Guide to the UN Agencies and Other Bodies

CCPI   Consultative Committee on Public Information for the UN. It deals with publicity and meets once a year.

ECA   Economic Commission for Africa. Encourages joint action to promote African commerce and gain a higher standard of living for Africans.

ECAFE   Economic Commission for Asia and the Far East. Promotes joint action to improve Asian commerce. See p. 113.

ECE   Economic Commission for Europe.

ECLA   Economic Commission for Latin America.

ECOSOC   Economic and Social Council. The main UN body dealing with economic and social questions. The four listed immediately above ECOSOC are all subsidiary to it.

FAO   The Food and Agricultural Organization. See p. 98.

FFHC   Freedom From Hunger Campaign, launched by FAO.

GATT   General Agreement on Tariffs and Trade. See p. 112.

IAEA   International Atomic Energy Agency. Promotes the use of atomic energy for peaceful purposes.

IBRD   International Bank for Reconstruction and Development. See pp. 112, 114.

ICAO   International Civil Aviation Organization. Deals with safety, standard procedures on international routes and at international airports.

ICEM   Intergovernmental Committee for European Migration. Organized and sometimes financed the transportation of refugees.

IDA   International Development Association. Connected with IBRD, it makes loans to developing countries.

IFAD   International Fund for Agricultural Development. It funds projects, in developing countries, which are designed to improve agriculture.

IFC   International Finance Corporation. Invests in suitable private enterprises in underdeveloped countries.

IMCO   Intergovernmental Maritime Consultative Organization. Welfare and safety at sea are its main concerns.

IMF   International Monetary Fund, also abbreviated to FUND. See p. 112.

ILO   International Labour Organization. See pp. 18, 95.

ITU   International Telecommunications Union. Much older than the UN itself, its aim is the co-operation of all nations in such matters as the use of cables, phones or satellites.

IUOTO   International Union of Official Travel Organizations. It has a loose, consultative connection with the UN.

ONUC   The UN military force in the Congo.

OPEX   Operational and Executive Personnel for Developing Countries. Opex men go to work for the governments of developing nations, and are paid by them. As experts, they train others to take over after them.

UNCTAD   United Nations Conference on Trade and Development.

UNDP   UN Development Programme. Aims to help the 'low income' countries realize their latent wealth. Works with the other UN agencies.

UNEP   The UN Environment Programme. It is concerned with all the world's pressing environmental problems, and arose from the UN Stockholm conference of 1972.

UNESCO   UN Educational, Scientific and Cultural Organization. See p. 110.

UNFICYP   UN Peace Keeping Force in Cyprus.

UNHCR   UN High Commissioner for Refugees. See p. 105. It co-ordinates and advises, but is not operational in the field.

UNICEF   UN International Children's Emergency Fund. See p. 115.

UNIDO   UN Industrial Development Organization.

UNRWA   UN Relief and Works Agency for Palestine refugees. See p. 105.

UPU   Universal Postal Union. See diagrams pp. 8, 94.

UNU   The UN University, established in 1973. Its work is to promote and assist research and training which will help towards the solution of some of the world's most pressing problems: world hunger, human and social development, and the use of natural resources. It has no campus, and does not award degrees, but works through a network of 'Associated Institutions' in member states.

WFC   The World Food Council, set up in 1973.

WFUNA   World Federation of UN Associations.

WFP   World Food Programme, put into action by FAO.

WHO   World Health Organization. See p. 99.

WMO   World Meteorological Organization. Controls weather forecasting and the exchange of weather information on a global scale.

Further Reading

F. P. WALTERS, *The League of Nations*, OUP.

C. L. MOWAT, *Britain Between The Wars*, Methuen.

G. M. GATHORNE-HARDY, *A Short History of International Affairs, 1919–39*, OUP.

E. H. CARR, *International Relations Between The Two World Wars*, Macmillan.

M. N. DUFFY, *The Twentieth Century*, Basil Blackwell.

S. BAILEY, *The United Nations*, Pall Mall Press.

K. SAVAGE, *The Story of the United Nations*, Bodley Head.

CORIOLANUS, *The Glass Lie*, W. H. Allen.

P. J. ROOKE, *The United Nations*, Blackie.

— *Your United Nations* (The Official Guide Book), UN Office of Public Information, New York.

— *Everyman's United Nations*, UN Office of Public Information, New York.

A. BOYD, *United Nations: Piety, Myth and Truth*, Penguin.

M. LEE, *The United Nations and World Realities*, Pergamon Press.

The other books in the *Modern Times Series* will provide useful information on the period covered by this book.

Index

Index

Index